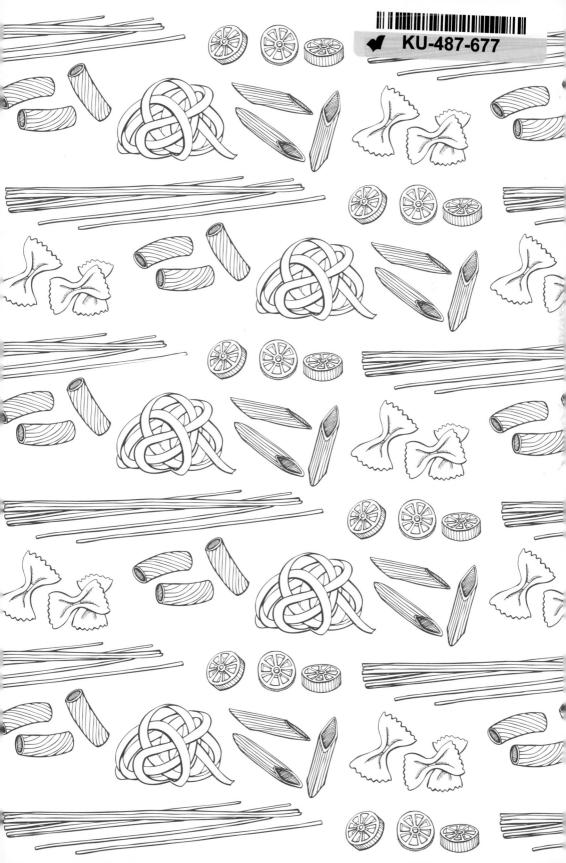

SKINNY PASTA

To my pillars of unconditional love and support,
my parents, Patricia and Franklin Azzarello.

SKINNY PASTA

80 flavour-packed recipes of less than 500 calories

Julia Azzarello

Photography by Tara Fisher

Kyle Books

An Hachette UK Company
www.hachette.co.uk

First published in Great Britain in 2018
by Kyle Books, an imprint of Kyle Cathie Ltd
Carmelite House
50 Victoria Embankment
London EC4Y 0DZ
www.kylebooks.co.uk

ISBN: 978 0 85783 4959

Distributed in the US by Hachette Book Group,
1290 Avenue of the Americas,
4th and 5th Floors, New York, NY 10104

Distributed in Canada by Canadian Manda
Group, 664 Annette St., Toronto, Ontario,
Canada M6S 2C8

Editor: Hannah Coughlin
Design: Louise Leffler
Photography: Tara Fisher
Food styling: Julia Azzarello
Props styling: Linda Berlin
Production: Nic John and Gemma Jones

A Cataloguing in Publication record for
this title is available from the British Library

Printed and bound in China

10 9 8 7 6 5 4 3 2 1

Notes

Standard level spoon measurements are used
in all recipes.
    1 tablespoon = one 15ml spoon
    1 teaspoon = one 5ml spoon

Eggs should be medium unless otherwise
stated. The Department of Health advises that
eggs should not be consumed raw. This book
contains dishes made with lightly cooked eggs.
It is prudent for more vulnerable people, such
as pregnant and nursing mothers, invalids, the
elderly, babies and young children, to avoid
uncooked or lightly cooked dishes made with
eggs. Once prepared these dishes should be kept
refrigerated and used promptly.

Pasta is dried unless otherwise stated.

Milk should be full fat unless otherwise stated.

Ovens should be preheated to the specific
temperature – if using a fan-assisted oven,
follow manufacturer's instructions for adjusting
the time and the temperature.

This book includes dishes made with nuts
and nut derivatives. It is advisable for those
with known allergic reactions to nuts and nut
derivatives and those who may be potentially
vulnerable to these allergies, such as pregnant
and nursing mothers, invalids, the elderly,
babies and children, to avoid dishes made with
nuts and nut oils. It is also prudent to check
the labels of pre-prepared ingredients for the
possible inclusion of nut derivatives.

Nutritional information key:
    DF – dairy-free
    GF – gluten-free
    V – vegetarian
    VE – vegan

Vegetarians should look for the 'V' symbol
on a cheese to ensure it is made with
vegetarian rennet.

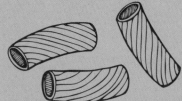

contents

introduction

Picture yourself in a beautiful mountain town nestled between the Amalfi Coast and the city of Naples. Wander down the road a little and smell and feel the fresh, salty sea air mingling with the cool mountain breeze. Look up, and you will see rows upon rows of pasta drying on rods and over balconies in this lovely medieval village. Now wake up.

In the town of Gragnano, the pasta capital of Italy in the Campania region, this used to be the only way to dry pasta, but these days you will not find it drying on balconies. It's a romantic tale of pasta's origins, which has become a favourite food throughout the world. Unfortunately, many who love pasta also fear it; with the rise of no-carb, low-carb, ketogenic and paleo(lithic) diets, pasta has become something of a dietary bogeyman.

In fact, pasta itself is not fattening, nor is it inherently bad for you. Italians have been eating it for centuries, and the Mediterranean diet is one of the world's healthiest, emphasizing fruits, vegetables, nuts, little meat and dairy and good oils, such as olive oil. Paired with the right sauce, pasta makes a healthy, well-balanced dish.

I eat and cook with whole foods; no fat-free products or artificial sweeteners. Nor do I believe in following food trends, the latest of which include using charcoal, matcha (green tea noodles are delicious, but that's another book) or turmeric in everything. They all have their place — like watermelon radishes — but that place is just not in pasta. Classics are around because they have withstood the test of time — like a pair of jeans worn with a crisp white shirt.

But the recipes in this book are not your Nonna's (grandmother's): they are lighter interpretations of classic Italian and European dishes and also less labour intensive, so you won't spend your day slaving over a saucepan of pork bones and tomatoes. Using only good-quality, flavourful ingredients, the calories are whittled down through clever swaps and portion sizes. Meat is used in moderation, or as an addition. Likewise, cream, butter and cheese are limited. These foods in themselves are not bad, it is only when they are consumed in extreme levels that they are harmful. Since most of us live busy lives, I've mostly relied on canned beans and lentils, dried pasta and stock cubes, but if you have homemade stocks around, feel free to use them — they will only enhance the flavour, especially in the soups.

Eating is one of life's great pleasures. I have spent months eating pasta for dinner, lunch and snacks while writing this book and I can honestly say that I am not tired of it. With so many combinations, the possibilities are endless. It also connects us: a recipe can be passed from one generation to the next, remaining a classic or subtly tweaked into something new.

You'll discover how to make fresh pasta and homemade sauces, how to incorporate pasta into comforting soups and ways to serve scrumptious pasta starters. And, of course, there are also plenty of classic pasta main-course dishes that you will be able to enjoy without feeling as though you have used all your calories for a week in one sitting! These recipes will show you that your favourite pastas can be enjoyed, guilt-free. Life is too short not to eat pasta!

cook's notes

Recipes

Read the recipe through and make sure you have all the ingredients in front of you before you commence cooking. I find it useful to prepare all my ingredients and place them in little bowls, ready to be cooked. The French call this *mis en place* and it is how great restaurants run so smoothly – all the ingredients are ready from the start. Aim to have the pasta and sauce ready at the same time; for sauces that take longer to make, wait until your sauce is almost completely cooked before boiling the pasta.

Ingredients

Make sure you buy the best quality ingredients you can afford. It truly makes a difference buying well-raised chicken, beef and dairy. Buy local produce whenever you can, as it will be fresh and have had to travel fewer miles from the farm to your plate. I've tried to limit sourcing ingredients to local shops and markets. Any obscure shapes of pasta can be purchased in your local Italian deli or online, or you can substitute a similar pasta shape.

Special diets

Most of the recipes in this book are adaptable – many can easily be made vegetarian or vegan by swapping or omitting the cheese, and any of the traditional durum wheat pastas can be swapped for gluten-free versions, of which there is now an abundance on the market. Quinoa, corn, rice, buckwheat, brown rice and amaranth are all gluten-free, though buckwheat is sometimes mixed with whole wheat, so check the label. The only ones I don't recommend are black bean and lentil pastas, because I find they have a very strange texture. It is a matter of experimenting to find one you like.

Seasoning

Use flaked sea salt, such as Maldon or Cornish, to season sauces, and coarse sea salt to flavour pasta water. I use 2 scant tablespoons to season pasta for a main course for 4, and half this quantity for starters. If I'm cooking less than 100g (3½oz) of pasta, I use 1 teaspoon of salt. Season the sauce in balance with the ingredients; if the recipe calls for capers and olives, for example, you will need to use less salt.

Pepper is best freshly ground. Fresh herbs are also preferrable, but you can easily substitute dried, just halve the quantity. Simiarly, you can substitute dried chilli flakes with fresh if you wish. To crush garlic, I chop the clove with a pinch of salt, then drag the side of a chef's knife back and forth until I have a paste. Although most chefs don't like them, you can use a garlic press instead if you wish.

pasta shapes and sauces

Every shape of pasta has its purpose, depending on the sauce that it's carrying. Italians take this very seriously, and would never serve spaghetti with meatballs or Bolognese for example as it's too thin. A long flat pappardelle or a short tubular rigatoni holds the chunky sauce better.

Long, thin pasta
Examples: spaghetti, linguine, vermicelli
Best with: tomato, oil, creamy sauces, sauces that are not too chunky, seafood, pesto

Tubular, long, broad pasta
Examples: penne, rigatoni, ziti, bucatini, pappardelle, tagliatelle
Best with: ragù, chunky meat or vegetable sauces, creamy sauces

Small shapes and tubes
Examples: acini di pepe, ditalini, broken capelli d'angelo (angel hair)
Best in: soups, casseroles, stews, salads

Curly, twisted odd shapes
Examples: fusilli, farfalle, orecchiette, conchiglie
Best with: pesto, chunky meats or veggies

cooking pasta

Measure at least 1 litre (35fl oz) of water to 100g (3½oz) of pasta; less water than this and the pasta will become a starchy, sticky mess. I use a 6-litre (6-quart) saucepan and fill it three quarters full with water. It is important to bring the water to the boil first, add the salt, stir, then add the pasta.

It is best to cook pasta until it is al dente (firm to the bite). Although cooking times are given, different pasta brands can vary in how long they need. Check the packet instructions and test it a minute or two sooner than the given time, as the pasta will continue to cook after it has been drained and mixed with the sauce.

When you drain pasta, reserve 100–150ml (3½–5fl oz) of the cooking water and add it to the sauce if it needs help amalgamating with the pasta.

Using pasta in soups

When using pasta in soups, I usually cook it in the soup and adjust the stock. If I'm storing the soup, I cook and store the pasta separately as the pasta tends to soak up a lot of the stock.

kitchen equipment

To make pasta dishes you'll need very little in the way of equipment – but you do need to use the correct ones. Just as you wouldn't paint your house with a watercolour brush, you wouldn't chop a butternut squash using a paring knife – a chef's knife will get the job done quicker and more efficiently. Every saucepan, knife and spoon has a purpose.

You don't need every gadget in the fancy cook's shops; they use up space and money. On the other hand, if you buy cheap, you buy twice. Invest in good-quality saucepans and knives – they are well worth the initial purchase, should last you a long time and often come with guarantees.

I've whittled down the list of kitchen equipment you need to these essentials:

Pots and Pans

A good stainless-steel tall and wide pasta saucepan, preferably with a fit-in colander. Size is important: there needs to be enough room for water to absorb into the pasta without it sticking together, so you'll need at least a 5–6 litre (5–6 quart) one. And it should be made from stainless steel, which won't affect the flavour of your food.

A large colander to strain pasta if you're using a saucepan without an insert.

A good, heavy-gauge, deep frying pan or sauté pan in which you can make sauces and toss with pasta in the same pan. I recommend getting one 30cm (12in) wide, 5cm (2in) deep.

A medium-heavy gauge saucepan about 20cm (8in) wide and 9cm (3½in) deep for sauces such as marinara or cheese sauce.

Baking Dishes and Trays

Baking dishes for casseroles and lasagnas. Good sizes to have are around 20cm (8in) or 23cm (9in) square, which will be perfect for serving 4–6.

Good-quality baking trays of about 39 x 27cm (15½ x 10¾in) in size. Choose heavy-gauge ones, which won't warp.

Silicone mats for roasting vegetables, to stop them sticking.

Utensils and Kitchen Tools

As well as the basics that all kitchens will have, there are a few pasta specific tools that will be helpful:

- Tongs or pasta spoon for serving
- A soup ladle
- Digital scales (for calorie precision)
- A food processor for pesto and soups
- A mortar and pestle for small-batch pesto and salsas
- A stand mixer for handmade pasta dough
- A rolling pin
- A manual pasta maker for ease of rolling, thinning and cutting pasta dough

pantry basics

The ingredients in this book can be bought at your local supermarket or farmers' market. A few of the pasta shapes are more obscure but can be found at Italian delis or online. Or you can always substitute a similar pasta shape. This list is a good pasta-making pantry foundation:

Vinegars

It's good to stock good-quality red wine and white wine vinegars for finishing dishes and making vinaigrettes. You should also have an aged balsamic vinegar, preferably from Modena with an acidity of 6%. A good aged balsamic vinegar can be pricey, but most shops will have a decent one that won't cost too much and, when used in moderation, it lasts a long time.

Olive oil

Virgin olive oil for cooking: none of the recipes in this book heat oil beyond its smoking point and the flavour is so lovely and fruity. Cold-pressed extra virgin olive oil is good for finishing dishes and vinaigrettes, as it is a purer olive oil than heat-extracted versions. It is a tad more costly, but worth it. To find your favourite olive oil, experiment with different brands. I like subtle, fruity and bright olive oils that are not too peppery. Always store it in a cool, dark place away from light and heat, and use within a year of the press date.

Capers

I like the small capers in vinegar, but capers in salt are wonderful as well, though make sure you rinse them well. Some capers are very tiny; if you are using larger ones, chop them roughly.

Anchovies

Choose salted anchovies packed in oil as they are boneless. Ortiz is a good brand. Beware, some anchovies can still have bones in that are tricky to remove.

Dried herbs

Dried herbs are great for when you can't get fresh ones. I keep in stock dried whole or flaked chillies, dried oregano, basil, parsley and rosemary.

Sea salt
Coarse sea salt is best to flavour pasta
water, but Maldon or Cornish Sea Salt
flakes are ideal for finishing and seasoning.

Whole Peppercorns
Always grind peppercorns as needed,
otherwise the flavour fades and dulls
too quickly. Tellicherry peppercorns are
ripened on the vine for longer than most
other varieties and develop a bit more zing.

Tomato purée
Double- or triple-concentrated tomato
purées pack a punch. Tubed tomato
concentrate makes for easy storage and use.

Canned tomatoes
If you can, look out for San Marzano
tomatoes. Mutti or Rega brands are lovely
and quite affordable.

Olives
Kalamata or black Spanish or Italian olives
are versatile, and Nocellara are lovely,
plump and fruity green olives.

Canned beans
Chickpeas, cannellini beans and borlotti
beans are a great basic bean selection for
any pantry.

Wine
Only cook with wine you would drink;
never use cooking wines as they are loaded
with too much salt. The quality is worth it.

Flours

00 flour — has a high protein content that will give pasta a bit more bite and chew. Plain flour will also work fine though.

Semola rimacinata — for egg-free pasta. It gives a grainier surface which holds sauce well. Made from durum wheat, it has a lovely flavour and yellow colour, and is milled to a finer consistency than semolina. It is higher in protein and gluten than 00 flour so is more durable.

Gluten-free flours — as a replacement for wheat flour. I have used brown rice, quinoa, corn and potato flours in this book's recipes.

Xanthan gum

Use this thickening agent for making gluten-free pasta.

Eggs

Choose medium, organic if possible, and weigh them to be more precise: eggs are usually 50–55g (1¾–2oz).

Breadcrumbs

Simply whiz stale bread in a food processor and store for a week or two in the fridge. You can also freeze for a few months.

Dried Pasta

Dried pasta comes in a variety of shapes (see page 10). Try to avoid anything cheap and shiny. Fregola, a Sardinian pasta, is particularly great for soups and has a lovely nuttiness. I like to keep at least a few long pastas, like spaghetti or angel hair, a few short-cut, such as rigatoni or farfalle, and some tiny for soups such, as ditalini and shells, in my pantry.

Fresh Produce

Onions and garlic are essential — yellow or white onions for sauces and red onions for salads. Fresh garlic is a must-have: the cloves should be firm and plump and the skin taught and not broken and flaking off. Smoked garlic is great for adding a lovely smoky essence to vinaigrettes and sauces and is widely available in supermarkets. Fresh juicy lemons are a great pantry staple — you should be able to get at least 2 tablespoons of juice from a good lemon. Where possible, use fresh herbs, such as basil, parsley, rosemary and oregano. If they are in pots, you can keep them alive on a windowsill, even in the cold months.

Cured Meats

Pancetta and thinly shaved Parma ham, speck and streaky bacon are good for adding a burst of flavour and texture.

Hard Cheeses

Parmesan Reggiano, Grana Padano, Pecorino or Sardo are the best cheeses to use with pasta. A little goes a long way, which is key when you're counting calories. It's always worth the effort to freshly grate cheese as it will be far more flavoursome.

Butter

Always use good-quality unsalted butter; cheaper ones contain more water.

Freezer Staples

Frozen peas, broad beans and sweetcorn are useful vegetables to stock in the freezer. Homemade stocks, if you've got them, are also good to freeze.

staples

This chapter contains staple recipes that you can refer to for dishes throughout the rest of the book, from basic pasta dough and classic sauces, to final flourishes of roasted tomatoes to top your dish. All the recipes here will work equally well with either shop-bought or home made pasta, so if you do have a little time on your hands, give making the pasta from scratch a go — included are a variety of basic doughs to try. The following sauces will provide a good base for many recipes, and if you make them in advance they will keep in the fridge for a quick and easy supper any day. Extra little touches, such as roasted tomatoes or peppers, can enhance any pasta dish, with a burst of flavour and a hit of colour. And an added bonus, there are no added preservatives or oils when you make them yourself, so they're even better for you.

basic fresh pasta dough

There is much debate about the best flour for making pasta; OO flour or pasta flour are preferrable, but plain flour works just as well. Your ingredients, the humidity and the temperature in the kitchen can all effect the outcome. Keep the flour bag and a bowl of water close so that you can easily add more flour or, if the dough needs more liquid, you can wet your hands. You may find you don't need to use all of the flour and that is fine too.

Serves 4
(makes 400–450g/14oz–1lb pasta)

 calories 337 DF V

Carbs 58g   Sugar 0.5g   Protein 13g   Fibre 3g   Fat 5g   Sat Fat 1.5g   Salt 0.2g

300g (10½oz) OO flour, plus extra for dusting
3 large eggs (150–160g/5 ½–5 ¾oz)

Place the flour on a clean, dry work surface, make a well in the centre and add the eggs. Using a fork, gather flour from around the edges, mixing until it comes together and you can use your hands to knead the dough. If it feels too dry, wet your hands. It takes practice, but you will get a feel for a good pasta dough. Knead for about 10 minutes until it is smooth and shiny. Alternatively, mix in a stand mixer fitted with a dough hook until it comes together. Cover and leave to rest in the fridge for 30 minutes.

Divide the dough into 4 equal-sized pieces and keep covered so they don't dry out. Take one piece, flatten it, and put it through the largest setting on the pasta maker. Fold it in thirds then push it through again, at least 3 times, then move down the level and repeat a few times.

Alternatively, roll the dough by hand. Shape one piece of dough into a flat oval and begin rolling from the centre away

from you. Roll and rotate to keep it even until it is as thin as a sheet of paper.

Either run the sheet through your cutter attachment of choice, or hand cut the dough into any shape you desire. For long shapes, flour well enough so it does not stick together.

Dust with flour and make into nests if using immediately. To store, drape the pasta over a wooden hanger and dry for a few hours, then keep in an airtight container in the fridge and for a few days. Alternatively, dry the pasta until it is brittle, a good 4–6 hours, then store in an airtight container and in a cupboard for 1 month.

To cook, bring a large pan of salted water to the boil. Add the pasta and cook until al dente. Thin spaghetti should not take longer than about 2 minutes; tagliatelle will need 3 minutes.

Note: for an eggless pasta follow the method above with 300g (10 ½oz) semola rimacinata and 130–140ml (4–5fl oz) water (at body temperature), with some extra for dusting and kneeding.

gluten-free tagliatelle

This has lovely nutty quinoa notes but is quite labour intensive, as it doesn't have gluten to provide stretch. It will fall apart at first, but be patient, and keep folding it back together: it will take at least a minute to come together — or about 8 times through the machine. Working in small batches makes this easier.

Serves 4 (makes 450g/1lb)   DF GF V

Carbs 59g Sugar 1.5g Protein 9g Fibre 2.5g Fat 7g Sat Fat 1g Salt 0.2g

100g (3½oz) brown rice flour, plus a little extra (25g/1oz) for dusting
100g (3½oz) quinoa flour
50g (1¾oz) cornflour
50g (1¾oz) potato flour
1 teaspoon xanthan gum
2 eggs (100g/3½oz)
60–70ml (4–5 tablespoons) water
1 tablespoon olive oil

In the bowl of a stand mixer fitted with a dough hook, sift all the flours and xanthan gum together. Slowly add the wet ingredients until the dough comes together. Knead for 5 minutes, then cover and rest in the fridge for 30 minutes.

Alternatively, make the pasta by hand. Mix the flours and xanthan gum together, then place on a clean, dry surface. Make a well in the centre and add the eggs, water and oil. Slowly mix together using a fork until you can knead the dough with your hands, then knead for about 5–10 minutes. Wet your hands if the dough feels too dry. Cover with clingfilm and leave to rest in the fridge for 30 minutes.

Divide the dough into 4 equal-sized pieces and cover. Flatten out 1 piece and begin to feed it through a pasta machine on the largest setting. It will fall apart, but gather it up and repeat about 8 times until it holds together. Fold it in thirds and run it through the machine again a few times, moving down settings. Stop at setting 2 as it may tear if it gets too thin. Pass it through your cutting attachment of choice.

Alternatively, roll the dough by hand. Shape one piece of the dough into a flat oval and begin rolling from the centre outwards. Roll and rotate the dough to keep it even until you have a thin sheet. Cut the dough into any shape you desire, being sure to flour well enough so it does not stick together.

Dust with flour and make into nests if using immediately. Leave to dry for a few hours draped over a wooden hanger, before storing in an airtight container in the fridge for a few days.

To cook, bring a saucepan of water to the boil, add salt and cook for 2–3 minutes, or until al dente.

gluten-free gnocchi

Shop-bought gnocchi is often dense and hard, but this recipe makes a light and airy version – wonderful little fluffy pillows of potato goodness!

Serves 4 (makes 550g)

Carbs 47g   Sugar 1.5g   Protein 6g   Fibre 3g   Fat 2g   Sat Fat 0.5g   Salt 0.3g

2 medium baking potatoes (600g/1lb 5oz), scrubbed
1 egg (50g/1¾oz), beaten
60–80g (2¼–2¾oz) gluten-free plain flour (80–100g/2¾–3½oz if using 00 flour)
20g (¾oz)gluten-free or 00 flour, for dusting

Preheat the oven to 200°C (400°F), Gas Mark 6.

Prick the potatoes with a fork and wrap them in foil. Bake them for an 1–1 hour 20 minutes, or until tender. Leave to cool slightly, for about 15 minutes, then scoop out the potato and pass through a ricer. You need about 400g (14oz). Mix in the egg and flour.

Dust a clean worktop with flour. Divide the dough into 4 equal-sized pieces. Roll each one out to a cylinder 20cm (8in) long, and cut into 2cm (¾in) chunks. Make grooves on each piece using the back of a fork, then place on a baking tray dusted with flour.

Bring a large saucepan of salted water to the boil and cook in two batches for 1 minute, or until they float to the top. Remove with a slotted spoon. If using immediately, just add to your sauce. If not, cool briefly in iced water then place on a plate lined with kitchen paper to drain excess water. Keep in a sealed container in the fridge, or freeze for 2-3 months.

spaetzle

These little egg noodles are very popular in Germany. They are simple to make and delicious with just a pat of butter and some herbs. I use them for my chicken soup recipe on page 74. You don't need to spend money on a fancy spaetzle maker: a hand grater or colander will do.

Serves 4 (makes 450g/1lb)

Carbs 42g   Sugar 1.5g   Protein 10g   Fibre 2g   Fat 4.5g   Sat Fat 1.5g   Salt 0.4g

210g (7½oz) plain flour
¼ teaspoon fine sea salt
2 eggs
110–120ml (3¾–4¼fl oz) whole milk

Mix all the ingredients together in a bowl until the batter is thick and drips slowly off the whisk. Try not to over whisk or the spaetzle will be tough. You may need to add more flour if the batter is too thin or more milk if it's too thick. Leave to rest, covered, for 45–60 minutes in the fridge.

Bring a saucepan of water to the boil and add salt. Prepare a bowl of iced water.

Lay a large-holed grater or a colander over the top of the pan. Place a ladleful of the batter onto the back of the grater or into the colander and rub it through the holes using a spatula, dropping little dumplings into the boiling water. They will float to the top when done, usually 1–2 minutes.

Once they are done, drop the dumplings into a bowl of iced water to prevent them sticking together. Continue to make the dumplings, using a ladleful of batter at a time, until all the batter is used up.

If you're using immediately, add to your chosen sauce and warm through to serve. Alternatively, drain the spaetzle and store in the fridge for use later.

marinara sauce

Marinara sauce can be made using fresh or canned tomatoes; use fresh only when you have the ripest, summer tomatoes as winter ones will prove to be dry and mealy. It is very satisfying to watch a whole tomato melt into a thick river of red sauce. Alternatively, use canned San Marzano tomatoes – a variety of plum tomato first grown in volcanic soil near Mount Vesuvius in the town of San Marzano sul Sarno, in Southern Italy, they are sweeter and less acidic than other varieties and have become the 'it' tomato of the culinary world. If you can't get hold of them, add a pinch of bicarbonate of soda to neutralize the acidity of the tomatoes rather than a pinch of sugar – a trick my great aunt used in family recipes.

Serves 4
(makes 700ml/1¼ pints)

 calories 67 DF GF V

Carbs 9g   Sugar 8.5g   Protein 3g   Fibre 2g   Fat 2g   Sat Fat 0.2g   Salt 1.3g

2 x 400g (14oz) cans chopped or peeled plum tomatoes, preferably San Marzano (add a pinch of bicarbonate of soda if using other tomatoes), or 1kg (2lb 4oz) ripe plum tomatoes
2 teaspoons olive oil
½ sweet onion, finely diced
2 garlic cloves, minced
1 tablespoon torn basil leaves
1 tablespoon fresh chopped oregano
1 tablespoon fresh chopped parsley
Pinch of chilli flakes
Salt and pepper

If you're using fresh tomatoes, first bring a saucepan of water to the boil and prepare a large bowl of iced water. Mark an X on the bottom end of each tomato using a sharp pairing knife. Once the water is boiling, drop the tomatoes into the water and leave for 1 minute. Once you see the skin start to peel away from the flesh, remove the tomatoes using a slotted spoon and drop them into the iced water. Peel away the skin and chop the flesh.

Heat the olive oil in a medium saucepan, add the onion and cook for 4–5 minutes, then add the garlic and cook for a minute.

Add the tomatoes, crushing any large pieces in your hand as you put them in the pan, and add the bicarbonate of soda, if using. Season with salt and pepper and simmer over a medium heat for 20–25 minutes, stirring frequently to avoid it catching. Add the herbs and chilli flakes and reduce for a further 10 minutes. If you only have dried herbs, add 1 teaspoon of each after cooking the garlic and cook for a further minute to infuse.

lean bolognese sauce

This can be made with lentils instead of pancetta and mince for a vegetarian version. Turkey mince is very lean and low in fat. At one time, you could only find turkey at the butcher at Christmas; now, most supermarkets carry all sorts of turkey options.

Serves 4
(makes 980g/2lb 3oz)

 calories 500

Carbs 63g   Sugar 10g   Protein 29g   Fibre 7g   Fat 11g   Sat Fat 5g   Salt 0.9g

50g (1¾oz) pancetta
1 onion, diced
1 celery stick, diced
1 carrot, peeled and diced
250g (9oz) 5% fat beef or turkey mince, or 200g (7oz) beluga lentils
100ml (3½fl oz) red wine
800g (1lb 12oz) plum tomatoes, preferably San Marzano, diced
300g (10½oz) pasta
Salt and pepper
40g (½oz) Parmesan, grated, to serve

Heat a large, deep frying pan, add the pancetta, onion, celery and carrot and cook for 5 minutes. Add the meat or lentils and cook for 3–4 minutes. Add the wine, cook for 1 minute, then add the tomatoes and season. Simmer for 20–25 minutes.

Meanwhile, cook your chosen pasta in boiling salted water, following the packet instructions, until al dente.

Add the pasta to the sauce and stir well. Serve topped with the grated Parmesan.

traditional pesto sauce

This is a classic version of pesto, but you could also play around with different combinations: try coriander, peanuts and soy sauce, or baby kale, basil and pistachio.

Serves 4
(makes 120g/4¼oz)

 calories 170 GF

Carbs 0.6g   Sugar 0.2g   Protein 3g   Fibre 0g   Fat 17g   Sat Fat 3g   Salt 0.1g

1 or 2 garlic cloves
15g (½oz) toasted pine nuts
25g (1oz) young tender basil leaves
70ml (2½fl oz) olive oil
25g (1oz) Parmesan or gluten- and dairy-free cheese, grated
Salt and pepper

Blitz the garlic and pine nuts in a small food processor with a pinch of salt.

Add the basil leaves and, with the processor running, slowly drizzle in the oil. You can make it as fine or as chunky as you like.

Stir in the cheese – it gives it a better texture – and add pepper to taste.

oven-dried tomatoes

The key to low-calorie cooking is to extract as much flavour from the ingredients as possible without adding too many more calories. This is a lovely way to bring out the sweetness of tomatoes; they caramelize as the sugars break down, leaving behind a burst of soft sweetness.

Serves 4–6
(makes 200g/7oz)

 calories 25 DF GF V

Carbs 3g   Sugar 3g   Protein 1g   Fibre 1g   Fat 0g   Sat Fat 0g   Salt 0g

400g (14oz) cherry tomatoes, sliced in half widthways

Preheat the oven to 160°C (325°F), Gas Mark 3.

Place a nonstick mat on a large baking tray and add the tomatoes, flesh side up. Bake for 45 minutes, until caramelized and still a bit soft.

Leave to cool, then place in a clean container and store in the fridge for up to 1 week.

oven-roasted peppers

Roasting peppers is so easy: you will pass by the jars of peppers in the supermarket aisle once you've cooked these! For a charred pepper, I love to place it over the open flame burner on my hob and cook it until it is black. Not everyone has a gas hob, so I've adapted an oven recipe.

Serves 4

 calories 25 DF GF V

Carbs 6g   Sugar 6g   Protein 1g   Fibre 3g   Fat 0g   Sat Fat 0g   Salt 0g

4 red peppers, halved, cored and deseeded

Preheat the oven to 220°C (425°F), Gas Mark 7.

Place the peppers, cut side down, on a baking tray lined with a nonstick mat and roast for 40 minutes.

Once cooled, peel away the skin. Use in a recipe or store with the juices in a jar or container in the fridge for up to 1 week.

lunches

I feel like lunch is overlooked as a meal. I often find myself eating standing up as I'm working — I'll grab something that's left over from a recipe I'm styling or I'll just pick on bits of fruit, nuts or anything else within reach. This chapter is meant to elevate lunch from the likes of a sad tuna sandwich and an apple, proving that it deserves some thought rather than simply dressing up last night's dinner. These dishes could also be great for special occasions, such the Vermicelli with Lobster (see page 40), which would make a wonderful birthday lunch. Put some thought into where you eat it; perhaps in the garden surrounded by budding flowers waking from their winter's nap on a lovely spring afternoon. Invite friends around to share Chicken Sausage with Roasted Grapes, Pumkpin and Fregola (see page 46) which is the perfect hearty, warming meal for after a brisk walk on a crisp Autumn day. These also can make wonderful starters or a pasta course before a larger main. Whatever the occasion, sit, relax and enjoy your lunch.

beetroot ravioli

If you love beetroot, this is for you. It's full-on earthy, which the sweet citrus of orange juice and zest complements so well. The deep, rich purple of the sauce draped over the shocking pink ravioli is absolutely stunning.

Serves 4
(4 ravioli per person)

calories
256

Carbs 22g   Sugar 6g   Protein 11g   Fibre 2g   Fat 13g   Sat Fat 8g   Salt 0.5g

For the Beetroot Pasta
30ml beetroot juice
60-70ml water at body
    temperature
175g semola rimacinata

For the Roasted Beetroot Sauce
2 beetroot, about 100g (3
    ½oz) each
1 teaspoon olive oil
½ teaspoon caraway seeds
Juice of ½ orange
1 tablespoon butter
Salt and pepper

For the filling
200g (7oz) ricotta
50g (1¾oz) soft goats' cheese
1 tablespoon chopped parsley
1 tablespoon chopped chives

To garnish
2 tablespoons chopped chives
2 sprigs of dill, stems removed,
    chopped
Zest of 1 orange

Preheat the oven to 200°C (400°F), Gas Mark 6.

To make the beetroot pasta, follow the method for Basic Fresh Pasta Dough (see page 20).

To make the sauce, place the beetroot onto a sheet of foil and sprinkle with the oil, caraway seeds, salt and pepper. Place more foil on top and fold up the sides to form a packet. Roast for 1 hour, then cool.

Peel the beetroot and roughly chop, then purée in a blender with the orange juice, adding a little water to thin it out. You want the consistency of passata. Season with salt and pepper. Set aside.

Mix all the filling ingredients together and season.

Divide the pasta dough by half. Cover one half and roll the other to 60 x 24cm (24 x 9in), then cut in half lengthways so you have two long thin rectangles. Space out 8 dollops of the filling (about 2 teaspoons each) evenly on one sheet, cover with the other sheet and press down. Cut into 8 ravioli and seal each well, pressing out any air bubbles and pinching the edges closed. Repeat to make 8 more ravioli (16 in total).

Bring a saucepan of water to the boil, add salt and cook the ravioli for 2–3 minutes, or until al dente. Drain into the sauce using a slotted spoon and mix through.

Heat the butter in a deep frying pan until slightly browned, add the beetroot sauce and warm through.

Serve 4 ravioli per person and garnish with herbs and orange zest.

fresh tagliatelle with truffles

This dish is so simple, it just involves boiling a saucepan of water,
melting some butter and tossing. The truffle is the hero here.
Be sure to get truffles from a reputable supplier. They are expensive,
but worth every penny in my opinion.

Serves 4
calories
311

Carbs 27g   Sugar 1.5g   Protein 10g   Fibre 1.5g   Fat 17.5g   Sat Fat 10.5g   Salt 0.6g

200g (7oz) fresh tagliatelle
4 tablespoons butter
50g (1¾oz) Parmesan, grated
Salt and pepper
20–30g (¾–1oz) fresh shaved
truffle, to serve

Bring a saucepan of water to the boil, add salt and cook
the pasta for 3–4 minutes, or until al dente.

Melt the butter in a large, deep frying pan. Once the
pasta is done, drain, then add it to the pan of butter
with a little pasta water and stir in 40g (1½oz) of the
Parmesan quickly, so it doesn't clump. Add a little
more pasta water if it's too dry. Season to taste.

Serve in bowls, scattered with the shaved truffle and
the remainder of the Parmesan.

pea and orzo risotto

Orzo tends to be a bit starchier than other tiny pastas so I thought
it would make a lovely risotto. It is also easier than using arborio rice,
as you don't have to stir it so vigilantly. The addition of pea shoots
at the end gives this a lovely, sweet crunch.

Serves 4 calories 439

Carbs 60g   Sugar 3.5g   Protein 17g   Fibre 6g   Fat 11g   Sat Fat 5g   Salt 1g

1 tablespoon olive oil
1 shallot, finely chopped
1 garlic clove, minced
300g (10½oz) orzo
100ml (3½fl oz) dry white
   wine
400ml (13½fl oz) vegetable
   or chicken stock
150g (5½oz) frozen peas
50ml (2fl oz) single cream
50g (1¾oz) ricotta salata or
   Pecorino Romano, grated
10g (¼oz) mint, chopped
4 sprigs of tarragon, chopped
Salt and pepper
40g (1½oz) pea shoots,
   to garnish

Warm a large, deep sauce pan, then add the oil and
shallot and cook for 3–4 minutes. Add the garlic and
cook for a further 1 minute.

Tip in the orzo and stir around for 1 minute, then
add the white wine. Once the wine has evaporated,
pour in the stock and bring to the boil, then reduce
to a simmer. The orzo should take about 9–10 minutes
to cook, but keep an eye on it and stir it occasionally
so it doesn't stick to the bottom of the pan.

When it is creamy and cooked, stir in the peas,
single cream, grated cheese and herbs and cook for
2 minutes. Adjust the seasoning to taste.

Serve in bowls, sprinkled with the pea shoots.

mini anelletti al forno

This pasta bake is served at Easter in Sicily and is traditionally made with a meat ragu sauce, but I've substituted a marinara sauce to make a lighter dish. To make it vegetarian swap in a suitable vegetarian cheese.

It can be cooked in individual moulds or in a dish. Leave it to sit for a good 15 minutes before serving and unmoulding.

Serves 4–6 calories 327

Carbs 37g   Sugar 6g   Protein 16g   Fibre 5g   Fat 12g   Sat Fat 6.5g   Salt 0.5g

175g (6oz) anelletti (tiny hoops)
500ml (18fl oz) Marinara Sauce (see page 26)
100g (3½oz) frozen peas
40g (1½oz) Pecorino Romano or Parmesan cheese, grated
125g (4½oz) grated provolone (if you can get it) or mozzarella
Salt and pepper

Preheat the oven to 200°C (400°F), Gas Mark 6.

Bring a large saucepan of water to the boil, add salt and cook the pasta for 1–2 minutes, or until al dente, then drain. Toss the pasta into the marina sauce, season with salt and pepper, add the peas and stir in half the grated cheeses.

Pour into a non stick 20cm (8in) pie dish, top with the remainder of the cheese and cover with foil.

Bake for 30 minutes, then uncover and bake for a further 10 minutes, or until beginning to brown on top. Leave to rest for 15 minutes before serving.

pytt i panna

This is a take on the Swedish hash dish, whose name means "little pieces in a pan". I've made a version with Gluten-free Gnocchi (see page 23) instead of potatoes, chorizo for smoky flavour and hot-smoked salmon in place of traditional roast beef.

Serves 4

calories 493 · DF · GF

Carbs 31g   Sugar 8g   Protein 25g   Fibre 5.5g   Fat 28.5g   Sat Fat 7g   Salt 1.8g

1 teaspoon olive oil
1 red onion, roughly chopped
2 carrots, peeled and diced
   into 15mm (⅝in) pieces
100g (3 ½oz) chorizo, diced
   into 15mm (⅝in) pieces
200g (7oz) plain hot-smoked
   salmon, cut into chunks
½ batch of Gluten-free
   Gnocchi (see page 23)
4 quail's eggs
2 tablespoons chopped dill
2 tablespoons chopped parsley
100g (3½oz) pickled beetroot,
   drained and diced

Vinaigrette
1 tablespoon white wine vinegar
½ teaspoon Dijon mustard
3 tablespoons olive oil
½ small shallot, finely diced
Salt and pepper

Heat a nonstick saucepan, then add the oil, onion and carrots and cook for 5–8 minutes. Add the chorizo, salmon and gnocchi and cook for a further 2–3 minutes.

Whisk all the ingredients for the vinaigrette together.

Fry the eggs in a separate nonstick pan over a medium heat for about 1 minute, ensuring the yolks are runny.

To serve, divide the gnocchi mixture among 4 plates, top each with a fried quail's egg, drizzle over the vinaigrette and scatter with the chopped herbs and diced beetroot.

vermicelli with lobster

I've added chervil, also known as French parsley, to this dish as I love its liquorice essence, which complements the Pernod. Sprinkle it on right at the end, as it's a delicate herb. Any good fishmonger will have cooked lobster; I wouldn't recommend frozen lobster, but at a pinch, crayfish tails will do instead. It is pure decadence without the guilt.

Serves 4 calories 370

Carbs 38.5g   Sugar 3.5g   Protein 15.5g   Fibre 3g   Fat 14.5g   Sat Fat 8.5g   Salt 0.5g

200g (7oz) vermicelli
500–600g (1lb 2oz–1lb 5oz) cooked lobster (150g/5½oz meat once cleaned)
40g (1½oz) butter
2 tablespoons Pernod
100ml (3½fl oz) single cream
25g (1oz) chervil, stems removed, chopped
Salt and pepper
1 lemon, cut into wedges to squeeze over pasta

Bring a large saucepan of water to the boil, add salt and cook the pasta for 8–9 minutes, or until al dente. Drain, reserving a little of the cooking water.

Crack the shell of the lobster, remove all the meat and cut into bite-sized pieces.

Melt the butter in a large, deep frying pan over a medium heat. Add the lobster and cook, stirring, for 1–2 minutes until warmed through. Add the Pernod, season with salt and pepper, and cook for 1 minute.

Add the cooked pasta and cream plus a splash of the pasta cooking water to the lobster. Stir in the chopped chervil, reserving a little for garnishing.

To serve, divide the pasta among 4 bowls and swirl it into a nest shape, then sprinkle with the remaining chervil and serve with lemon wedges.

southern-style prawns in angel hair nests

This dish is inspired by Lee Bailey's New Orleans cookbook from the early '90s, but to me, it's timeless. I often prepared this for my clients when I was a personal chef so I've adapted it over the years, and here even more so to lower the calories. I've used shelled prawns for ease of eating. It has Creole flavours, from the French and Spanish occupation, as well as Native American and African influences. New Orleans is a magical, almost haunting place. I hold several fond memories of its people, but even more of its cuisine. Be sure to visit if you ever get the chance.

Serves 4 calories 391 DF

Carbs 41.5g   Sugar 5g   Protein 18g   Fibre 3g   Fat 16.5g   Sat Fat 8.5g   Salt 1.7g

250g (9oz) or 24 raw, peeled king prawns, patted dry
2 teaspoons creole spice mix (Waitrose make a good one)
2 teaspoons vegetable oil
2 spring onions, thinly sliced
1 garlic clove, minced
4 tablespoons Worcestershire sauce
Zest and juice of 1 lemon
4 tablespoons cold butter, diced
200g (7oz) capelli d'angelo ("angel hair") nests
Salt and pepper
Thyme leaves, to garnish
1 lemon, cut into wedges, to serve

Sprinkle the prawns with the creole spice mix and some salt and pepper. Warm 1 teaspoon of the oil in a large, nonstick frying pan and sauté the prawns for 2–3 minutes. Remove and set aside.

Add the remaining 1 teaspoon of oil to the pan, add the spring onions and cook for 1–2 minutes, then add the garlic and cook for a further 1 minute. Stir in the Worcestershire sauce and lemon zest and juice, then whisk in the butter. Return the prawns to the pan. Drain off 3 tablespoons of the sauce and reserve to drizzle.

Cook the pasta in a pan of boiling salted water for 2–3 minutes then drain and toss in the pan to coat everything with the sauce.

To serve, divide the pasta among 4 small dishes and form little nests, top with the prawns and the remainder of the sauce. Garnish with thyme leaves and serve with lemon wedges.

beef and mushroom stroganoff with pappardelle

Beef Stroganoff, named after the 18th-century nobleman Count Pavel Aleksanrovich Stroganoff, is the ultimate comfort food. It is usually made with a tough cut of meat and braised for hours at a low temperature. But there's no need to wait hours for this one to get to the table: I've made a quick version using grilled sirloin and chestnut mushrooms. I've also slimmed it down for a guilt-free dining experience.

Serves 4 calories 500

Carbs 41g   Sugar 4.5g   Protein 54g   Fibre 4g   Fat 13g   Sat Fat 5g   Salt 1.3g

200g (7oz) pappardelle
1 teaspoon vegetable oil
1 onion, thinly sliced
200g (7oz) chestnut
   mushrooms, quartered
1 teaspoon sweet paprika
1 tablespoon tomato purée
2 teaspoons Dijon mustard
1 beef stock cube dissolved in
   200ml (7fl oz) boiling water
2–3 tablespoons soured cream
2 x 400g (14 oz) sirloin steaks,
   trimmed of fat
Salt and pepper
2–3 tablespoons parsley,
   to garnish

Bring a large saucepan of water to the boi and add salt. Add the pasta and cook for 9–10 minutes, or until al dente. Drain, reserving some of the cooking water.

Meanwhile, warm a deep frying pan over a medium heat, then add the oil and onion and cook for 5 minutes. Add the mushrooms and cook for a further 5 minutes. Add the paprika, tomato purée, mustard and stock and cook for 2 minutes, then remove from the heat and stir in the soured cream.

Season the steaks and grill for 3 minutes per side, leave to rest for 5 minutes, then slice against the grain.

Toss the pasta and sauce together and serve on plates with the steak slices. Garnish with parsley.

butternut squash nests with ham, burrata and rocket

Crisping the Parma ham not only brings out its wonderful deep and rich character but also adds a lovely crunch to this starter, as well as cooking off some of the fat without losing any of the flavour. I love all the textures going on in this dish; tender pasta is combined with crunchy rocket and Parma ham and a smooth, creamy cheese.

Serves 4 calories 341

Carbs 23.5g   Sugar 4g   Protein 15g   Fibre 2.5g   Fat 20.5g   Sat Fat 8g   Salt 1.3g

70g (2½oz) Parma ham

200g (7oz) butternut-squash noodles,these can be made on a spiralizer, but luckily they are available in packages from most supermarkets.

100g (3½oz) capelli d'angelo ("angel hair") nests

1 tablespoon olive oil

1 tablespoon butter

2 garlic cloves, minced

2 sage leaves

40g (1½oz) rocket

125g (4½oz) burrata or buffalo mozzarella, quartered

40g (1½oz) Oven-dried Tomatoes, (see page 29)

4 teaspoons aged balsamic vinegar of Modena

2 tablespoons extra virgin olive oil

Salt and pepper

Chilli flakes, to garnish

Preheat the oven to 180°C (350°F), Gas Mark 4.

Place the ham on a nonstick baking tray and cook for 5 minutes. Turn it over and cook for an additional 10 minutes, or until very crispy. Remove and place on kitchen paper to absorb the fat. Crumble the ham and set aside until needed.

Bring a large saucepan of water to the boil, add salt, then add the squash noodles and cook for 3–4 minutes. Add the angel hair nests and cook for a further 1–2 minutes. Drain the squash and pasta and set aside.

Heat the oil and butter in a medium frying pan, add the garlic and cook for 1–2 minutes. Add the squash and pasta to the pan along with the sage and cook for a further 1–2 minutes. Season to taste.

Make a bed of rocket on 4 plates, divide the squash and pasta between the plates and form into little nests. Top with some burrata and tomatoes and sprinkle with Parma ham bits. Drizzle balsamic vinegar and extra virgin olive oil over each dish and garnish with chilli flakes and freshly ground black pepper.

chicken sausages with roasted grapes, pumpkin and fregola

Roasting grapes really brings out their essence and leaves behind a sweet, syrupy juice that mingles with the sausages, giving you a lovely sweet and salty balance. Paired with the nutty fregola and pumpkin, it is a wonderful autumnal dish.

Serves 4

Carbs 46g   Sugar 15g   Protein 26g   Fibre 4.5g   Fat 9.5g   Sat Fat 2g   Salt 1.3g

350g (12oz) pumpkin or butternut squash flesh, diced
2 teaspoons olive oil
8 Italian chicken sausages
½ red onion, sliced
150g (5½oz) red seedless grapes, snipped into little clusters
150g (5½oz) fregola
1 sprig of rosemary, leaves chopped
Salt and pepper
2 tablespoons extra virgin olive oil, to drizzle
4 tablespoons aged balsamic vinegar of Modena, to drizzle

Preheat the oven to 220°C (425°F), Gas Mark 7.

Toss the pumpkin or squash with 1 teaspoon of the oil and some salt and pepper in a roasting tin. Bake for 15–20 minutes.

Meanwhile, warm an ovenproof 28cm (11in) frying pan and add the remaining oil and the sausages. Cook for 3 minutes, turning the sausages as they brown, then add the onion and grapes and cook for a further 2 minutes. Transfer to the oven and bake for 10 minutes.

Bring a large pan of water to the boil, add 1 teaspoon of coarse salt and cook the fregola for 6–8 minutes, or until al dente, then drain.

Toss the pumpkin or squash, rosemary and fregola together and divide among 4 shallow bowls. Place the sausages and some onions and grapes on top, then drizzle over the extra virgin olive oil and balsamic vinegar and serve.

salads

Salads are one of my favourites meals. My husband never used to eat them until I showed him the wonder of using more than just lettuce, tomatoes and a bottled ranch dressing. The ingredient palette is endless with influence from culture and seasonal ingredients.

A salad can be a healthy lunch with loads of crunchy vegetables to get you through the day. It can be a hearty dinner even in the winter months with roasted root vegetables and leftover roasted chicken. You can mix up different vinegars, oils and spices to suit your salad. Salads are starters, sides, mains or just a lovely way to stave off hunger when you are feeling peckish.

They can also be a wonderful way to lighten pasta dishes. Think about textures when creating your salad. What is the foundation ingredient? What dressing will complement the components? Does it need something crunchy on top? Play around with the following recipes and create your own versions.

'panzanella' salad with spelt pasta

The authentic version of this Tuscan salad is a good way to use up tomatoes and stale bread, but I've replaced the bread with spelt pasta. Spelt is easier to digest than wheat pasta as it has a bit less gluten. Salting the tomatoes releases their juice into the dressing, which is soaked up by the warm pasta.

Serves 4

Carbs 23g   Sugar 5g   Protein 5g   Fibre 3.5g   Fat 11.5g   Sat Fat 2g   Salt 1.5g

500g (1lb 2oz) heirloom or sweet cherry tomatoes, mixed colours if possible

2 teaspoons sea salt flakes

100g (3½oz) spelt pasta, or any other short-cut pasta, such as penne or rigatoni

¼ white sweet onion, sliced

60g (2¼oz) black olives, such as Kalamata, pitted and chopped

For the vinaigrette

3–4 tablespoons extra virgin olive oil

1 tablespoon good-quality red wine vinegar

1–2 smoked garlic cloves, minced or crushed (or use regular garlic)

1 teaspoon Dijon mustard

½ teaspoon sea salt

To garnish

3 tablespoons chopped parsley leaves

handful of picked Greek basil leaves or regular small basil leaves

Pepper, to taste

Cut the tomatoes into bite-sized chunks, place in a colander over a large bowl and toss with the salt flakes. Leave to sit for 15 minutes, tossing occasionally.

Bring a pan of water to the boil, add salt and cook the pasta until al dente, about 9–10 minutes. Drain, but do not cool.

Meanwhile, make the vinaigrette by putting all the ingredients into a jar and shaking vigorously until it comes together.

Add the vinaigrette to the bowl of drained tomato juice, then add the tomatoes, warm pasta, onion and olives and toss well.

Serve up on plates and garnish with the parsley, basil and pepper.

greek fusilli pasta salad

Greek Salad is a staple dinner for my family in the summer.
I love the crunch of the peppers, the coolness of the cucumber, and the
way the creamy feta cheese soaks up the sharp vinegar. The pasta is not
traditional, but makes a lovely addition here.

Serves 4

Carbs 34g   Sugar 7.5g   Protein 10g   Fibre 5g   Fat 20g   Sat Fat 6g   Salt 0.9g

200g (7oz) cherry tomatoes,
  on the vine
150g (5½oz) fusilli
8 Kalamata olives, pitted and
  roughly chopped
½ cucumber, halved
  lengthways, then sliced
½ red onion, sliced
1 red pepper and 1 green
  pepper, cored, deseeded and
  cut into 2cm (¾in) chunks
1 tablespoon good-quality red
  wine vinegar
4 tablespoons cold-pressed
  extra virgin olive oil
100g (3½oz) feta, crumbled
2 tablespoons each chopped
  dill, mint and parsley leaves
Salt and pepper

Preheat the oven to 200°C (400°F), Gas Mark 6.

Put the tomatoes, still on the vine, on a baking tray
and roast for 8–10 minutes, or until their skin cracks.

Meanwhile, cook and drain the pasta in a pan of
boiling salted water for 8–10 minutes until al dente,
then drain and rinse under cold water.

Toss the tomatoes, pasta, olives, cucumber, onion and
peppers together with the vinegar and oil. Season with
salt and pepper to taste.

Divide between serving plates and top each with some
of the crumbled feta. Scatter over the chopped herbs
and serve.

gemelli and summer vegetables with avocado and coriander sauce

I've used avocado in this vegan-friendly sauce for a creamy texture. These lovely little twists of pasta hold the sauce well. A dash or two of chilli sauce to finish balances out the richness of the avocado with a hit of heat and sharpness. The sugar snap peas and sweetcorn add just the right balance of sweetness. You can spoon the sauce into a jar and take it on a picnic or to work for lunch, but eat it on the day you make it, as the avocado will discolour.

Serves 4

Carbs 51g   Sugar 5g   Protein 11g   Fibre 7g   Fat 16g   Sat Fat 3g   Salt 0.6g

250g (9oz) gemelli
100g (3 ½oz) sweetcorn
  kernels
100g (3 ½oz) sugar snap peas,
  halved
150g (5 ½oz) cherry tomatoes,
  halved
Salt and pepper
Coriander leaves, to garnish
2 spring onions, sliced
Dash of hot sauce (e.g. Tabasco
  or Cholula)

For the sauce
1 avocado
1 or 2 garlic cloves
½ teaspoon sea salt
3–4 tablespoons lime juice
2 tablespoons olive oil or
  avocado oil
20g (¾oz) coriander leaves

Bring a saucepan of water to the boil, add salt and cook the pasta for 10–12 minutes, or until al dente. Add the sweetcorn and sugar snap peas 1 minute before the pasta is cooked. Drain and rinse under cold water.

To make the sauce, peel and pit the avocado and put the flesh into a food processor with the garlic, salt and lime juice. Blend until smooth, then add the oil and coriander and pulse a few times. Adjust the seasoning to taste.

Put the pasta, sweetcorn and sugar snap peas into a large bowl, add the tomatoes and sauce and mix.

Garnish with coriander leaves and spring onions and serve with a dash of hot sauce.

caprese pasta salad

This makes a lovely side salad for fish or grilled chicken and
is very quick and easy to prepare. It is also great for a picnic as it celebrates
summertime, when tomatoes and berries are at the peak of their flavour.
I've added strawberries and balsamic vinegar to give an extra sweetness – and
as a throwback to the '90s. Just grab your picnic rug
and a glass of Prosecco!

Serves 4

Carbs 40g   Sugar 5g   Protein 12.5g   Fibre 4g   Fat 21g   Sat Fat 6.5g   Salt 0.3g

200g (7oz) farfalle

300g (10½oz) heirloom
   tomatoes, cut into bite-sized
   wedges

100g (3½oz) strawberries,
   hulled and halved

125g (4½oz) bocconcini or
   mini mozzarella balls, each
   cut in half

70ml (2½fl oz) extra virgin
   olive oil

1 tablespoon good quality red
   wine vinegar

Salt and pepper

To serve

25g (1oz) basil leaves, torn, or
   a few handfuls of Greek basil
   leaves

Drizzle of aged balsamic
   vinegar of Modena

Bring a saucepan of water to the boil, add salt and cook
the pasta for 7–9 minutes, or until al dente. Drain and
rinse under cold water.

In a large bowl, toss together the pasta, tomatoes,
strawberries, bocconcini or mozzarella, olive oil and
red wine vinegar. Season to taste with salt and pepper.

Divide among 4 plates, scatter over the basil and drizzle
with balsamic vinegar.

creamy crayfish tails and pasta over cos lettuce

The first time I had crayfish was in New Orleans, where my friend
and I bought them boiled with Old Bay seasoning, garlic and lemons.
The aroma was so inviting I wanted to eat them on the spot.
Luckily we got delayed on the way home, so we cracked them open
using our hands and sucked the flesh out of the tail.
Sweet, delicate and juicy, they are like shrunken lobster.

Serves 4  calories 350

Carbs 35g   Sugar 8g   Protein 13g   Fibre 3.5g   Fat 16g   Sat Fat 4g   Salt 0.1g

150g (5½oz) chifferi rigati
(shell-shaped pasta)
200g (7oz) cooked crayfish tails
½ cucumber, diced
2 spring onions, thinly sliced
on an angle
Pinch of chilli flakes (optional)
½ mango, flesh diced
2 baby cos lettuces, leaves
separated
Salt and pepper
2 tablespoons extra virgin olive
oil, to drizzle
1 lemon, cut into wedges,
to serve

For the dressing
150g (5½oz) Greek yogurt
2 tablespoons mayonnaise
1 tablespoon white wine vinegar
1 tablespoon each chopped
chives, mint and dill
½ teaspoon caster sugar
Salt and pepper

Bring a saucepan of water to the boil, add salt and
cook the pasta for 5–6 minutes, or until al dente.
Drain and rinse under cold water.

Mix all the ingredients for the dressing together,
season, and set aside.

In a large bowl, toss the pasta, crayfish, cucumber,
spring onions, chilli flakes (if using) and mango
together with the dressing.

Arrange 3 or 4 lettuce leaves on each plate. Top with
the salad, drizzle with the olive oil and serve with the
lemon wedges.

buckwheat noodles with apple, smoked mackerel and red onion

Not all buckwheat noodles are gluten-free; some, like the ones I use here, contain wholemeal flour. I prefer the texture of these as I find pasta made with 100% buckwheat is a bit rubbery. Mackerel is a great source of omega 3 oil, which is good for maintaining a healthy heart and glowing skin.

Serves 4 calories 400

Carbs 25g   Sugar 6g   Protein 17g   Fibre 3g   Fat 25g   Sat Fat 4g   Salt 1g

100g (3½oz) buckwheat pasta
   noodles (not gluten-free)
1 small red apple, skin on,
   cored
1 celery stick
80g (2¾oz) watercress
¼ red onion, thinly sliced
200g (7oz) smoked mackerel
   fillet, flaked
30g (1oz) toasted sunflower
   seeds

For the dressing
100ml (3½fl oz) buttermilk
2 tablespoons mayonnaise
1 tablespoon olive oil
1 tablespoon lemon juice
1 teaspoon wholegrain mustard
1 garlic clove, crushed
2 tablespoons chopped chives,
   half reserved for garnishing
2 tablespoons chopped dill,
   half reserved for garnishing
Salt and pepper

Bring a large saucepan of water to the boil, add salt and cook the pasta for 3–4 minutes, or until al dente. Drain and rinse under cold water, then set aside.

Slice the apple into matchstick-sized pieces and place in a bowl of cold water until needed.

Shave or slice the celery stick and place into cold water until needed.

Make the dressing by whisking together all the ingredients, reserving half of the herbs for garnishing.

Drain the apple and celery. Arrange the watercress on individual plates, then arrange the noodles, apple, celery, onion and mackerel on top. Drizzle with the dressing and garnish with the sunflower seeds and remaining herbs.

tuna niçoise salad bowl

This is a brilliant way to get your veggies and protein in at lunchtime for slow-release energy. I use fresh tuna and cook it until it's still very pink inside. Be sure to buy from a trusted source to ensure it's as fresh as can be. Canned tuna will do at a pinch, or you can replace the tuna with cooked Puy lentils for a vegetarian version.

Serves 4

Carbs 30g   Sugar 3.5g   Protein 42g   Fibre 4g   Fat 15g   Sat Fat 3g   Salt 0.9g

150g (5½oz) quinoa or amaranth penne

100g (3½oz) French or green beans

2 eggs

500g (1lb 2oz) fresh yellowfin tuna steaks

2 Baby Gem lettuces, leaves separated

6 French breakfast radishes, sliced in half lengthways

60g (2¼oz) Niçoise olives

4 sprigs of tarragon, to garnish

For the vinaigrette

3 tablespoons olive oil

1 tablespoon white wine or tarragon vinegar

1 teaspoon Dijon mustard

1 sprig of tarragon, leaves chopped

Salt and pepper

Bring a saucepan of water to the boil, add salt and cook the pasta for 8–9 minutes, or until al dente. About 3 minutes before it's done, add the beans to cook. Drain and rinse under cold water and separate the beans from the pasta.

Bring a small saucepan of water to the boil and cook the eggs for 6 minutes. Rinse under cold water, peel and slice in half.

Season and cook the tuna steaks in a nonstick pan or grill pan for 2 minutes per side. Leave to rest, then slice thickly across the grain.

Make the vinaigrette by putting all the ingredients into a clean jar and shaking vigorously.

Arrange a layer of lettuce leaves in the bottom of each bowl, then top with the tuna, pasta, eggs, veggies, tomatoes and olives. Dress with the vinaigrette and garnish with the tarragon sprigs.

camaje salad with ceci pasta

Years ago, I worked at Camaje Bistro in the West Village of NYC with my friend, chef and owner Abigail Hitchcock. I lived on this salad for dinner every night. Her version has chickpeas in it, but I've substituted ceci (chickpea) pasta instead and added some herbs and smoked rapeseed oil. It is a go-to salad in my house when I'm tired of cooking, because it requires barely any effort. Thanks for the inspiration, Chef Hitchcock!

Serves 4

calories 449 · DF · GF

Carbs 25g   Sugar 6g   Protein 11g   Fibre 6.5g   Fat 33g   Sat Fat 6g   Salt 1.5g

100g (3½oz) ceci (chickpea pasta)
4 streaky bacon rashers
½ red onion, thinly sliced
½ large cucumber, cut into 2cm (¾in) dice
200g (7oz) heirloom or cherry tomatoes, halved
110g (3¾oz) rocket or mixed salad leaves
10g (¼oz) parsley, leaves picked
2 sprigs of tarragon leaves picked
2 avocados, pitted and sliced

For the vinaigrette
2 tablespoons smoked rapeseed oil
1 tablespoon olive oil
1 tablespoon sherry vinegar
1 tablespoon water
1 teaspoon Dijon mustard
1 teaspoon runny honey
1 garlic clove, smashed to a paste
½ teaspoon sea salt

Bring a saucepan of water to the boil, add salt and cook the pasta for 6 minutes, or until al dente. Drain and rinse under cold water.

Cook the bacon in a frying pan for 3 minutes per side, or longer if you like it extra crispy. Remove and drain on kitchen paper, then roughly chop.

Make the vinaigrette by putting all the ingredients into a clean jar and shaking vigorously.

In a bowl, toss together all the salad ingredients, except the avocados and bacon, with the dressing.

Divide among 4 plates and top each with fanned-out avocado slices and bacon bits.

chicken caesar salad

I adore both pasta and Caesar salad so I've combined them here for a light lunch or dinner. The dressing uses anchovies and Worcestershire sauce for an extra tangy umami that really lifts the dish. Always make sure you balance fats (oils) and acids (vinegar or lemon juice, for example) in your dressings. Instead of bread croutons, I've crisped pasta to sit atop the salad.

Serves 4  calories 420

Carbs 20g   Sugar 2.5g   Protein 29g   Fibre 2g   Fat 23g   Sat Fat 5.5g   Salt 1g

100g (3½oz) paccheri rigati
   (large pasta tubes)
1 tablespoon olive oil
1 garlic clove, minced
1 tablespoon chopped parsley
2 streaky bacon rashers
2 heads of Romaine or large
   Gem lettuces
250g (9oz) roasted chicken
   breast, sliced into strips
Salt and pepper, to taste
Lemon wedges, to serve

Dressing
40g (1½oz) Parmesan, grated
   (reserve half for sprinkling)
1–2 garlic cloves, smashed to
   a paste
3 anchovies, tinned in oil
   and drained
3 tablespoons olive oil
Zest of 1 lemon
3–4 tablespoons + 1 teaspoon
   lemon juice
1 tablespoon Worcestershire
   sauce
1 tablespoon mayonnaise
1 teaspoon Dijon mustard

For the pasta croutons, bring a saucepan of water to the boil, add salt and cook the pasta for 11–12 minutes, or until al dente. Drain and leave to cool.

Heat the olive oil in a nonstick frying pan and cook the pasta for 4 minutes per side, flipping as it cooks, until golden. Add the garlic at the last minute. Remove from the heat and sprinkle with the chopped parsley and some pepper.

Cook the bacon in a separate frying pan for about 3 minutes per side, then drain on kitchen paper and chop.

Combine all the dressing ingredients with seasoning in a blender.

Slice the lettuces in half lengthways and fan out on plates, top with the chicken, then pour over the dressing. Scatter over the pasta "croutons", bacon bits and the remaining Parmesan. This is best served straight away, while the croutons are freshly made, with lemon to squeeze over.

duck breast with radicchio, toasted walnuts and fregola

This salad is wonderful on a crisp autumn day. Agrodulce is an Italian sweet and sour sauce, which together with the juicy duck and bitter greens creates a perfect balance of taste sensations. The vinegar could be swapped for white wine or cider varieties, and you could try honey in place of the maple syrup.

Serves 4 calories 400

Carbs 23g   Sugar 11g   Protein 23g   Fibre 2g   Fat 15g   Sat Fat 4g   Salt 0.3g

60g (2¼oz) fregola
2 Gressingham duck breast
   portions (skin on), 125g
   (4½oz) each
3 heads of Radicchio, red or
   yellow chicory, treviso or
   anything similar
30g (1oz) walnuts, toasted and
   chopped
50g (1¾oz) pomegranate seeds
30g (1oz) blue cheese,
   crumbled
2 tablespoons cold-pressed
   extra virgin olive oil
Salt and pepper

For the agrodulce
125ml (4fl oz) red wine vinegar
60ml (4 tablespoons) maple
   syrup
Pinch of chilli flakes

Preheat the oven to 200°C (400°F), Gas Mark 6.

First make the agrodulce. Put the vinegar, syrup and chilli flakes in a pan and reduce for 6–8 minutes until syrupy. Set aside.

Bring a medium saucepan of water to the boil, add a teaspoon of salt and the fregola, and cook following the packet instructions (usually about 6–8 minutes). Drain through a sieve and run under the cold tap to cool. Set aside until you are ready to assemble the salad.

Pat the duck breasts dry with kitchen paper, then score the duck fat and season with salt and pepper. Cook, skin side down, in an ovenproof frying pan over a medium heat for 6–8 minutes until golden and the fat is rendered, then flip over and cook for a further 1 minute. Drain off the fat and transfer to the oven for a further 3–4 minutes, depending on your desired doneness. Remove from the oven to rest for at least 5 minutes and then slice thinly.

Slice the radicchio/chicory root ends into thin rings and quarter the rest of the heads lengthways.

Layer the raddichio/chicory on a platter or individual plates, then top with the fregola, duck, walnuts, pomegranate seeds and blue cheese. Drizzle with the agrodulce and olive oil and season with salt and pepper to taste. Serve.

soups

Soup is like an old friend. No matter if you are bundled up in a woolly blanket with a steaming cupful, or at a picnic surrounded by green grass and buttercups, pouring chilled soup from a thermos, soup comforts and nourishes. I recommend using homemade stock for the soup recipes if you have it. However, it is so easy to buy good-quality ready-made stock from the shops if you don't have time to make it. At a pinch, the cubes or condensed pots will work as well. Soups like Minestrone are a good way to use up loose vegetables from the fridge, see page 68, or they can turn a left over bit of meat into a new meal, like in the Pea and Pasta Soup with Ham on page 81. Not just for leftovers though, soups can also be served for special occasions, such as the Italian Wedding Soup on page 79.

The addition of pasta to soup adds texture and flavour. There are so many tiny pasta shapes on the market now too which are ideal for simmering in a broth. I find I make soups more often in the winter months, but a chilled soup can be wonderful in the summer as well.

minestrone soup

Minestrone is such a versatile soup. It is basically an assortment
of vegetables, some sort of bean and pasta. In Liguria, minestrone
is topped with pesto. This is a Ligurian version with borlotti beans,
other regions use cannellini or white beans. This version uses mostly
winter vegetables; try it in the spring with asparagus and broad beans.
In the summer, try it chilled.

Serves 4 calories 350

Carbs 41.5g   Sugar 11g   Protein 13g   Fibre 10.5g   Fat 12.5g   Sat Fat 1g   Salt 2.2g

1 tablespoon olive oil
1 onion, diced
1 carrot, peeled and diced
2 celery sticks, chopped
100g (3½oz) red potato,
   peeled and diced
2–3 garlic cloves, minced
150g (5½oz) courgette, diced
400g (14oz) can chopped
   tomatoes
1.4 litres (2½ pints) water or
   vegetable stock
400g (14oz) can borlotti beans,
   drained and rinsed
100g (3½oz) tiny pasta shells
100g (3½oz) green beans, cut
   into 2.5cm (1in) lengths
100g (3½oz) cavolo nero
Salt and pepper
4 tablespoons Traditional Pesto
   Sauce (see page 25), to serve

Warm a soup saucepan over a medium heat and add the
oil. Add the onion, carrot, celery and potato and cook
for about 8–10 minutes, stirring until golden. Add the
garlic and courgette and cook for 2 minutes. Add the
tomatoes and water or stock and simmer, uncovered,
for 25 minutes. Then add the borlotti beans.

Stir in the pasta and cook for 7 minutes, adding a
little more water or stock if needed. Add the green
beans and cavolo nero and cook for a further 5
minutes. Adjust the seasoning to taste.

Divide among 4 soup bowls and serve each with
a tablespoon of pesto swirled into the soup.

roasted garlic soup

I love garlic and make this when I feel as if I may be coming down
with a cold, as it is antibacterial. I'm not sure if it really cures me, but it
does make me feel recharged. My little girl once told me that she likes my
food because, "First you start with love, then you add the garlic". Both this
soup and my Instagram name, First love, then Garlic, are inspired
by my sweet Isla-Sophia.

Serves 4 calories 266

Carbs 30g   Sugar 3g   Protein 7g   Fibre 4.5g   Fat 9g   Sat Fat 3g   Salt 0.9g

2 large bulbs of garlic
2 tablespoons olive oil
1 large leek, white and light
  green parts only, trimmed,
  cleaned and sliced
1 small potato (100g/3½oz),
  peeled and diced
125ml (4fl oz) dry vermouth
  or sherry
1.4 litres (2½ pints) chicken
  stock
Bouquet garni (3 parsley stems,
  1 sprig of rosemary, 2 sprigs
  of thyme and 1 bay leaf, tied
  together with string)
50ml (2fl oz) single cream
100g (3½oz) ditalini or other
  small pasta, e.g. shells
Salt and pepper

To serve
 2 sprigs of thyme, leaves picked
Drizzle of aged balsamic
  vinegar of Modena

Preheat the oven to 200°C (400°F), Gas Mark 6.

Cut the tops off each bulb of garlic and toss with
1 tablespoon of the oil and some salt and pepper.
Cover in foil and roast for 1 hour until golden.
Squeeze the garlic flesh out of each clove and set
aside for later.

Heat a soup saucepan, add the remaining 1 tablespoon
of oil and sauté the leek and potato for 5 minutes. Add
the vermouth or sherry and cook for 5 minutes.

Pour in the stock, add the bouquet garni and simmer,
uncovered, for 15 minutes.

Remove the bouquet garni and add the roasted garlic
flesh. Purée the soup using a stick blender, then stir
in the cream.

Add the pasta and cook for 5 minutes.

Serve in bowls, scattered with thyme leaves and drizzled
with balsamic vinegar.

chickpea and broken noodle soup

This is a classic Roman soup and, as with many classic dishes, there are many variations on it. Canned beans make a quick version of the recipe, and it is a good way to use up those abandoned random bags of pasta from the cupboard. I like to blend some of it so it has a creamy texture, but feel free to skip this step.

Serves 4 calories 310

Carbs 42g   Sugar 5g   Protein 15g   Fibre 10g   Fat 7g   Sat Fat 2g   Salt 1g

1 teaspoon olive oil
1 onion, diced
2 celery sticks, diced
1 carrot, peeled and diced
2 garlic cloves, minced
1 tablespoon tomato purée
2 x 400g (14oz) cans chickpeas,
    drained and rinsed
1.4 litres (2½ pints) chicken or
    vegetable stock
1 sprig of rosemary, leaves
    chopped
100g (3½oz) broken tagliatelle
Salt and pepper
20g (¾oz) Pecorino Romano
    cheese, grated

Heat the oil in a soup saucepan over a medium heat, then add the onion, celery and carrot and cook for 8 minutes, stirring often so as not to burn.

Add the garlic and tomato purée and cook for 2 minutes. Add the chickpeas and stock and simmer, uncovered, for 25–30 minutes.

Remove about 300ml (10fl oz) of the soup, add the rosemary to this and purée, then add this back to the pan and bring to the boil. Add the pasta and cook for a further 10 minutes. Adjust the seasoning to taste.

Divide the soup among 4 bowls and serve sprinkled with the grated cheese.

fast bouillabaisse with tiny macaroni

I had never eaten, or indeed heard of, Bouillabaisse until I went to cooking school in my early twenties where I learned to make it: the shellfish broth was quite labour intensive, but worth it. I've used shop bought seafood stock here to cut down on labour, but not flavour.

Serves 4 calories 326 DF

Carbs 23g   Sugar 9g   Protein 25g   Fibre 4g   Fat 14.5g   Sat Fat 1.5g   Salt 1.2g

1 tablespoon olive oil
1 onion, diced
1 small fennel bulb, thinly sliced
1 garlic clove, crushed
400g (14oz) chopped tomatoes
1.4 litres (2½ pints) shellfish
  stock
Bouquet garni (see Note)
Zest of ½ orange
Pinch of saffron threads
200g (7oz) cod or haddock
  loin, cut into large chunks
70g (2½oz) fregola
100g (3½oz) cooked, peeled
  tiger prawns
100g (3½oz) fresh mussels,
  shell on, cleaned
2–3 tablespoons chopped
  parsley, to serve

For the rouille
3 tablespoons mayonnaise
1 garlic clove, crushed
Zest and juice of 1 lemon
½ roasted red pepper from a jar
  or homemade, see page 29
Dash of Tabasco sauce
Pinch of saffron threads
Salt and pepper

Heat a soup pot over a medium-high heat, add the oil and cook the onion and fennel for 5 minutes, then add the garlic and cook for a further 2 minutes.

Add the tomatoes, stock, bouquet garni, orange zest and saffron and simmer, uncovered, for 20 minutes.

Add the cod or haddock and fregola to the broth and cook for 3 minutes, then add the langoustines and cook for 2 minutes. Add the mussels, cover and cook for a further 2–3 minutes, until the fregola is al dente and the mussels have opened. Remove the bouquet garni.

Meanwhile, make the rouille. Put all the rouille ingredients into a small food processor or mortar and pestle, and blend to a purée.

Serve the soup in shallow bowls, topped with a dollop of rouille and some chopped parsley.

Note: You can either buy bouquet garnis pre-made, or easily make your own by tying 3 parsley stems, 2 sprigs of thyme, 1 sprig of rosemary and 1 bay leaf together with string.

chicken soup with spaetzle and dill

I love dill in chicken soup. My friend Adrienne, who had been an avid cook in her youth but, when I knew her, couldn't stand for long durations due to failing health, taught me to make her Jewish chicken soup. She always added parsnips and dill, which created the sweetest broth. Ever since, I add dill and think of the lovely Adrienne instructing me from her chair in her sunlit kitchen. She passed a few years ago, but her soul lives on every time I make her soup. This is a much simpler and quicker version — we used to cook a whole large saucepan of chicken and veggies for a few hours — but it still has the dill!

Serves 4 calories 255

Carbs 27g   Sugar 4.5g   Protein 24g   Fibre 3.5g   Fat 4.5g   Sat Fat 1.5g   Salt 1g

I teaspoon vegetable oil

4 spring onions, white and green parts separated and sliced

I small carrot, peeled and diced

I small parsnip, peeled and diced

2 garlic cloves, minced

300g (10½oz) boneless, skinless chicken breast halves

I litre (1¾ pints) chicken stock

½ recipe of spaetzle (see page 24), or 100g (3½oz) shop-bought spaetzle (if you can't find it, tiny bow pasta works nicely)

Salt and pepper

To serve

I tablespoon chopped dill

I tablespoon chopped parsley

Heat a soup saucepan over a medium heat, add the oil, the whites of spring onions, the carrot and parsnip and cook for 3 minutes. Add the garlic and cook for another I minute. Add the chicken and stock and simmer, uncovered, for 15 minutes, or until the chicken is cooked through.

Remove the chicken and shred the meat, then add it back to the saucepan. Adjust the seasoning to taste, add the spaetzle and cook for 2–3 more minutes.

Serve sprinkled with the herbs and green parts of the spring onions.

tomato soup with prosciutto cappelletti and basil

As a kid, I loved dunking my toasted cheese sandwiches into my tomato soup (in fact, I still do!). I used this inspiration but swapped the sandwich for cappelletti filled with prosciutto and cheese. To make this vegetarian, use a suitable cheese cappelletti. I love the way the centre of the smoky cappelletti melts in your mouth, mingling with the tang of the tomato, balancing the flavour out nicely.

Serves 4

Carbs 19g   Sugar 7g   Protein 6g   Fibre 2g   Fat 4.5g   Sat Fat 1g   Salt 0.4g

1 tablespoon olive oil
1 sweet onion, chopped
3 whole garlic cloves, crushed
  with a knife, then peeled
400g (14oz) can plum
  tomatoes
Zest of 1 orange and juice of ½
1 litre (1¾pints) water
2 sprigs of basil
200g (7oz) fresh cappelletti
  with prosciutto
Salt and pepper
A few basil leaves, to garnish

Warm a soup saucepan over a medium heat and add the oil and onion. Cook for 5 minutes, or until soft and golden, then add the garlic and cook for 2 minutes. Add the tomatoes, orange zest and juice and water, and simmer, uncovered, for 15 minutes.

Blend using a stick blender or pour into a stand blender. If you want your soup to be super smooth, pass it through a sieve or food mill. Adjust the seasoning to taste and add the basil, then give it another blend. Return the soup to the pan and keep warm over a very low simmer.

Meanwhile, boil a large saucepan of water, add the cappelletti and cook for 2–3 minutes, then drain.

Serve the soup in bowls, top with the cappelletti and garnish with a few basil leaves.

Italian wedding soup

I grew up on this Italian-American soup, and of course each family has their own special version of it. And yes, it is served at some weddings! The meatballs are traditionally made of beef, veal and pork, but I have lightened them with turkey breast mince. You could use 200g (7oz) lean beef and 200g (7oz) veal and it would still be within the calorie count. In the States, I use escarole to garnish, but in the UK you can substitute frisée.

Serves 4 calories 352

Carbs 18g   Sugar 5g   Protein 46g   Fibre 3g   Fat 10g   Sat Fat 3.5g   Salt 2.3g

1 tablespoon olive oil
1 sweet white or yellow onion, finely diced
1 celery stick, finely diced
1 carrot, peeled and finely diced
2 garlic cloves, minced
1 litre (1¾ pints) fresh chicken stock, preferably homemade
400g (14oz) minced turkey breast or 200g (7oz) minced lean beef and 200g (7oz) minced veal
1 egg
¼ teaspoon each dried oregano, basil and parsley
40g (1½oz) Pecorino Romano cheese, grated
70g (2½oz) acini di pepe (resembles tiny beads)
Salt and pepper

To serve
40g (1½oz) frisée or shredded escarole
4 tablespoons chopped parsley

Heat a soup saucepan over a medium heat, then add the oil, onion, celery and carrot. Cook for 5 minutes, stirring until golden. Add the garlic and cook for a further 1 minute. Pour in the stock and simmer, uncovered, for 10 minutes.

Mix the minced turkey or beef and veal, the egg, dried herbs, 20g (¾oz) of the cheese and some salt and pepper together and roll into tiny meatballs about 2.5cm (1in) in size. (You should have about 16 meatballs.)

Add the meatballs to the soup and simmer, uncovered, for 10 minutes. Add the acini di pepe and cook for 5 minutes; you may need to adjust the stock and add a little extra.

Serve in soup bowls, sprinkled with the remaining grated cheese and topped with the frisée or escarole and parsley.

pasta y fagiole

The small addition of pancetta gives this a lovely smoky essence, but it can be left out, and the chicken stock eliminated, if you want a vegetarian version. I grew up on pasta y fagiole: it was a staple of my mother's winter soup repertoire. I've since added fennel because I love its liquorice essence and texture.

Serves 4 calories 417

Carbs 46g   Sugar 8g   Protein 30g   Fibre 13g   Fat 9.5g   Sat Fat 4g   Salt 1.5g

75g (2¾oz) diced pancetta
1 sweet onion, finely diced
2 celery sticks, finely diced
1 carrot, peeled and finely diced
1 small fennel bulb, stalks and fronds removed (save fronds for garnishing), finely diced
2 garlic cloves, minced
200g (7oz) canned chopped tomatoes, or chopped fresh if in season
2 x 400g (14oz) cans cannellini beans, drained and rinsed
1.4 litres (2½ pints) chicken stock or water
1 bay leaf
1 sprig of rosemary, leaves chopped
100g (3½oz) ditalini or other small pasta, e.g. shells
¼ teaspoon chilli flakes
Salt and pepper

To serve
40g (1½oz) rocket
20g (¾oz) Parmesan, grated

Add the pancetta to a soup saucepan and place over a medium-high heat. Stir for 4 minutes, until golden, then remove half of the pancetta using a slotted spoon and set aside.

Add the onion, celery, carrot and fennel to the pancetta and rendered oil remaining in the saucepan and cook for 5 minutes, stirring. Add the garlic and cook for 1 minute, then add the tomatoes, beans, stock or water and bay leaf and simmer, uncovered, for 40 minutes over a low heat.

Remove the bay leaf and add the rosemary. Purée half of the soup then return it to the pot. Add the ditalini and chilli flakes to the soup and cook for 8 minutes, adding a little more stock if needed. Adjust the seasoning to taste.

Divide among 4 bowls and garnish with the rocket, Parmesan and reserved pancetta.

pea and pasta soup with ham

This is a super simple soup you can throw together for a last-minute lunch or dinner. It couldn't be easier, yet it is still homemade. The salty and smoky ham make the perfect base for the sweet and tender peas.

Serves 4

calories
307

Carbs 33g   Sugar 2g   Protein 25g   Fibre 4.5g   Fat 7.5g   Sat Fat 4g   Salt 1.8g

1.4 litres (2½ pints) chicken stock
150g (5½oz) gemelli
200g (7oz) leftover cooked smoked ham, diced
200g (7oz) frozen peas
Salt and pepper

To serve
50g (1¾oz) Parmesan, grated
2 tablespoons each of chopped mint and chopped parsley

Bring the stock to the boil in a soup saucepan, add the pasta and cook for 7–8 minutes, or until al dente.

Add the ham and peas and simmer, uncovered, for 5 minutes. Adjust the seasoning to taste.

Serve in bowls, sprinkled with the grated Parmesan and chopped herbs.

butter bean, chorizo and spinach soup with pappardelle

This recipe was inspired by a trip to Seville, where I could not get enough of chorizo. I love the way they deglaze it with vinegar: it really cuts through the oils of the chorizo and makes it less slick in the mouth. Spanish cuisine traditionally uses chickpeas in a lot of dishes, but I've used butter beans here instead as I love their rich and creamy texture.

Serves 4 calories 314

Carbs 33g   Sugar 7g   Protein 16.5g   Fibre 8.5g   Fat 11g   Sat Fat 4.5g   Salt 1.7g

100g (3½oz) cooking chorizo, sliced

2 tablespoons red wine vinegar

1 leek, white and light green parts only, trimmed, cleaned and thinly sliced

1 garlic clove, sliced

1 tablespoon smoked sweet paprika

400g (14oz) can chopped tomatoes

400g (14oz) can butter beans, drained and rinsed

1 litre (1¾ pints) chicken stock

100g (3½oz) pappardelle, broken

125g (4½oz) spinach

Salt and pepper

To serve

1 green chilli, thinly sliced, seeds and all

A few coriander leaves

4 tablespoons Greek yogurt

Heat a soup saucepan over a medium heat and sauté the chorizo for 2 minutes, until beginning to crisp. Add the vinegar and cook for a further 1 minute, then remove the chorizo with a slotted spoon, drain on kitchen paper and set aside until needed.

Add the leek to the saucepan and cook for 5 minutes, then add the garlic and paprika and cook for a further 3 minutes. Pour in the tomatoes, butter beans and stock and simmer, uncovered, for 10 minutes.

Tip in the pasta and cook for 4 minutes, then add the spinach and stir through for 1 minute. Adjust the seasoning to taste.

Pour the soup into 4 bowls, divide the chorizo among the bowls and top with the chilli, coriander leaves and a dollop of yogurt on each.

veggie mains

With the rise of Meat-free Mondays and Flexitarian eating comes a plethora of delicious plant-based food, and the recipes in this chapter are a great way to pack more veggies into your diet. Not all of them are strictly vegetarian, as many use Parmesan, so swap this for an alternative vegetarian hard cheese if you prefer — there are plenty available in supermarkets nowadays.

If you can, try to eat vegetables with the seasons. This guarantees peak freshness and flavour. Take corn for example, it is at is best in the months of August to September. The husk is a lovely green, the silk is fresh and the entire cob is firm. The kernels are bursting with juice that is so sweet you don't even need to butter or salt them. Eat it out of season, and you won't even find it in the husk and the kernels are tough, chewy and bland. For example, Spring brings the arrival of broad beans, peas and asparagus, which constitute Mafaldine Pasta Prima Vera on page 122. Certain vegetables seem to be always available like cauliflower, certain cabbages, button mushrooms and herbs. Fresh herbs add so much depth to a dish along with a zing of colour, like the Linguine Lunghi with Herbs, Green Olives and Lemon on page 106. Luckily for us, many vegetables such as corn, broad beans and peas freeze well, meaning they can be used all year round. The versatility of vegetables is endless. You can roast and bring out a sweetness hidden within, steam, or simply sauté with a touch of olive oil. The romanesco on page 102 breaks down to form a creamy sauce that is full of flavour and not calories. Have fun and use these recipes as a guideline to come up with some of your own combinations.

fresh pappardelle with roasted cauliflower and creamy mustard sauce

I love the sharpness that mustard provides to this sauce. It cuts through the rich cauliflower and cream balancing it out on the tongue. Cauliflower is such a hero vegetable that deserves to play a leading role in most dishes instead of sitting beside a baby carrot on a vegetable platter.

Serves 4 calories 485

Carbs 62g   Sugar 11.5g   Protein 21g   Fibre 8g   Fat 14g   Sat Fat 6g   Salt 3.5g

1 large cauliflower (1kg/2lb 4oz), broken into florets

3 teaspoons olive oil

2 teaspoons sea salt

1 sweet onion, thinly sliced

2 tablespoons bourbon

1 tablespoon wholegrain mustard

1 teaspoon Dijon mustard

1 chicken stock cube dissolved in 350ml (12fl oz) boiling water

350g (12½oz) fresh pappardelle

100ml (3½fl oz) single cream

20g (¾oz) Parmesan, grated

2 tablespoons chopped parsley

Black pepper

Preheat the oven to 200°C (400°F), Gas Mark 6.

Toss the cauliflower florets with 2 teaspoons of the oil and the sea salt and spread out on two baking trays. Cover with foil and roast for 20 minutes. Remove the foil and roast for a further 10–15 minutes, or until golden. Remove and set aside, covered, until needed.

Bring a large saucepan of water to the boil and add salt.

Heat a frying pan, add the remaining oil and the onion, cook for 8–10 minutes over a medium-high heat, stirring until golden brown. Add the bourbon and simmer for 1 minute, then add the mustards and stock and simmer for 5 minutes.

Add the pappardelle to the saucepan of boiling salted water and cook for 3 minutes, or until al dente. Drain, reserving some of the pasta water.

Slowly whisk the cream into the pasta sauce, then tip in the pasta and roasted cauliflower and toss. Add a little of the reserved pasta water to loosen the sauce if needed.

Serve on 4 warm plates and sprinkle with the grated Parmesan, chopped parsley and some pepper.

fusilli with trapanese pesto

This is the Sicilian version of pesto and is best made in the summer when tomatoes are in the height of their season: it's delicious but worth making only if you use lovely sweet ripe tomatoes.

Serves 4 calories 474

Carbs 61g   Sugar 5g   Protein 17g   Fibre 5g   Fat 17g   Sat Fat 4g   Salt 0.8g

30g (1oz) whole blanched almonds
320g (11¼oz) fusilli
2 garlic cloves, peeled
½ teaspoon sea salt
350g (12oz) cherry tomatoes
25g (1oz) basil leaves
3 tablespoons olive oil
40g (1½oz) Pecorino Romano, grated
Salt and pepper

Preheat the oven to 180°C (350°F), Gas Mark 4.

Put the almonds on a baking tray and toast in the oven for 7–8 minutes, until golden. Remove and leave to cool.

Meanwhile, bring a saucepan of water to the boil, add salt and the fusilli and cook for 9–11 minutes, or until al dente. Drain.

Meanwhile, put the garlic and measured salt in a food processor and pulse until minced. Add the nuts and pulse until coarse. Add the tomatoes and basil and whizz while slowly adding the olive oil until a coarse paste is formed. Stir in three-quarters of the cheese. Adjust the seasoning to taste.

Add the pesto to the warm pasta and serve sprinkled with the remaining cheese.

macaroni and cheese

I don't think I'm alone in claiming that macaroni and cheese is the
ultimate comfort food. It conjures memories of independence for me
as I remember when, aged 11, I prepared it all by myself for dinner.
It may have been from a box, but watching the cheese sauce magically
come together and tasting it was so satisfying. Now, of course,
I make it all from scratch as it is quite simple.

Serves 4 calories 500

Carbs 46g   Sugar 2.5g   Protein 22.5g   Fibre 3g   Fat 3g   Sat Fat 15g   Salt 1.9g

215g (7½oz) macaroni, chifferi
rigati or shell-shaped pasta
25g (1oz) butter
2 tablespoons plain flour
½ vegetable stock cube
dissolved in 250ml (9fl oz)
boiling water
100ml (3½fl oz) semi-
skimmed milk
1 tablespoon Dijon mustard
100g (3½oz) Cheddar cheese,
grated
100g (3½oz) smoked Gouda
cheese, grated
15g (½oz) Pecorino Romano,
grated
2 tablespoons chopped parsley
Salt and pepper

Bring a large saucepan of water to the boil, add salt
and cook the pasta for 7 minutes, or until al dente.

Meanwhile, in a saucepan, melt the butter, then stir in
the flour and cook for 1 minute. Slowly add the stock
and milk, stirring until combined before adding more
liquid. Cook for 2 minutes until thickened (it won't
be super thick), then stir in the mustard, Cheddar and
Gouda. Cook only until the cheese is melted, about
30 seconds, so as not to clump or split.

Drain the pasta and stir it into the cheese sauce. Adjust
the seasoning to taste. Serve immediately, topped with
the grated hard cheese and chopped parsley.

Note: If you're making it ahead of time, cook the pasta
for only 5 minutes. You can also place it under the grill
to brown if you like. To reheat, add a splash of stock
or milk, tip into an ovenproof dish, cover and place in
the oven preheated to 180°C (350°F), Gas Mark 4 for
20–30 minutes.

rigatoni with fresh cherry tomatoes and olives

This dish came together from foraging through my pantry and fridge one evening. This type of meal can be a bit hit or miss, but this was definitely a hit. The sugary, tart cherry tomatoes blend with the meaty, savoury olives and fragrant basil to create a lovely pasta dish.

Serves 4 calories 493

Carbs 57g   Sugar 5g   Protein 14g   Fibre 6g   Fat 21g   Sat Fat 4.5g   Salt 0.8g

300g (10½oz) rigatoni or other short-cut pasta
4 tablespoons olive oil
5–6 garlic cloves, thinly sliced
400g (14oz) cherry tomatoes, halved
100g (3½oz) mixture of Picholine, Nocellara and Kalamata olives or whatever you have on hand, pitted and roughly chopped
Salt and pepper

To serve
40g (1½oz) Parmesan, grated
15g (½oz) basil leaves, thinly sliced (chiffonade)

Bring a saucepan of water to the boil, add salt and cook the pasta for 12–14 minutes, or until al dente. Drain, reserving some of the pasta water.

Meanwhile, warm 2 tablespoons of the oil in a frying pan and cook the garlic for 2 minutes. Remove with a slotted spoon and set aside.

Add the tomatoes to the pan and cook for 5 minutes, then add the pasta and olives and return the garlic to the pan, along with a little pasta water. Cook for 3 minutes.

Serve drizzled with the remaining olive oil and sprinkled with the grated Parmesan, sliced basil and some pepper.

cannelloni with spinach and herbed ricotta

I use quite a bit of sauce in this as the pasta is baked not boiled and needs the liquid to soak up. A bit of sauce on the side is nice as well. You can experiment with different fillings. Minced meat works well for meat lovers and kale or Swiss chard can be substituted for the spinach.

Serves 4 calories 488

Carbs 46g   Sugar 10g · Protein 28g   Fibre 5g   Fat 21g   Sat Fat 11g   Salt 2g

200g (7oz) baby spinach
250g (9oz) ricotta
2 large eggs, beaten
5 sprigs of parsley, leaves
  chopped
1 sprig of oregano, leaves
  chopped
12 cannelloni tubes
1 quantity Marinara Sauce
  (see page 26)
125g (4 ½oz) mozzarella,
  grated
20g (¾oz) Parmesan, grated

To serve
5 basil leaves, torn
Pepper

Preheat the oven to 200°C (400°F), Gas Mark 6.

Warm a large frying pan with 1 tablespoon of water. Add the spinach, cover the pan and steam for 30 seconds. Stir until wilted. Cool, then squeeze the water from the spinach and chop.

In a bowl, mix together the spinach, ricotta, parsley, oregano and eggs. Place in a piping bag and pipe evenly into the cannelloni tubes.

Make the marinara sauce and set aside about one-third for serving. Add a few tablespoons of sauce to the bottom of a baking dish about 28 x 20 x 5cm (11 x 8 x 2in) in size. Add the stuffed cannelloni, pour over more marinara sauce and scatter with the mozzarella cheese. Cover with foil and bake for 30 minutes, then uncover and brown for 10–15 minutes.

Just before the cannelloni are cooked, reheat the remaining marinara sauce. Serve 3 cannelloni per person, topped with more sauce and sprinkled with the Parmesan, the torn basil and some pepper.

conchiglie pasta and vodka sauce

This is a dish that found popularity in the 1970s in America. Vodka, used instead of wine, gives the sauce a smooth flavour. Classically, it is paired with penne, but I like to use conchiglie, the shell-shaped cut instead. The sauce gets trapped inside each shell and bursts in your mouth.

Serves 4 calories 491

Carbs 68g   Sugar 11g   Protein 18g   Fibre 4g   Fat 10g   Sat Fat 5g   Salt 0.4g

1 teaspoon vegetable oil
2 garlic cloves, minced
½ teaspoon dried chilli flakes
   (optional)
90ml (6 tablespoons) vodka
800g (1lb 12oz) passata
100ml (3½fl oz) single cream
300g (11¼oz) conchiglie
Salt and pepper

To serve
40g (1½oz) Parmesan, grated
Handful of basil leaves, torn
   if large

Warm a large, deep frying pan, add the oil and cook the garlic for 1–2 minutes. Add the chilli flakes, if using, and the vodka and cook for 1 minute. Pour in the passata and adjust the seasoning with salt and pepper. Simmer for 15 minutes, then slowly whisk in the cream.

Meanwhile, bring a saucepan of water to the boil, add salt and cook the pasta for 10 minutes, or until al dente, then drain.

Toss the warm pasta and sauce together. You shouldn't need to add any pasta cooking water as it is quite saucy.

Serve with the Parmesan and basil leaves.

creamy fettuccine with garlic and herbs

What could be better than butter, cream and cheese mixed with pasta? Not much as far as I'm concerned. Just because you are watching your calorie intake, it doesn't mean you need to deprive yourself entirely: this dish still comes in at under 500 calories per serving.

Serves 4 calories 451

Carbs 59g   Sugar 2.5g   Protein 15.5g   Fibre 4.5g   Fat 16g   Sat Fat 9.5g   Salt 0.4g

320g (11¼oz) fettuccine
2 tablespoons butter
3 garlic cloves, minced
100ml (3½fl oz) single cream
Few grates of nutmeg
50g (1¾oz) Parmesan, grated
1 tablespoon chopped parsley
1 tablespoon chopped chives
5 basil leaves, torn
Salt and pepper

Bring a saucepan of water to the boil, add salt and cook the fettuccine for 8 minutes, or until al dente.

Meanwhile, melt the butter in a large, deep frying pan, then add the garlic and cook for 1 minute. Stir in the cream and grated nutmeg, then slowly whisk in 40g (1½oz) of the grated Parmesan.

Drain the pasta, reserving some of the cooking water. Add the pasta to the sauce and toss in the herbs. If the sauce is too thick, thin it out with a little pasta water.

Serve immediately, sprinkled with pepper and the remaining grated Parmesan.

farfalle and caponata

I love the combination of sweet and sour flavours with soft and crunchy textures in this Sicilian sauce. It's classically served with rich meats, such as lamb, to cut through the fat, or with meaty fish, such as swordfish. I've paired it here with pasta to create a great vegan dish.

Serves 4

Carbs 75g   Sugar 18g   Protein 13g   Fibre 10g   Fat 11g   Sat Fat 1.5g   Salt 0.4g

1 medium aubergine (about 450g/1lb), cut into 2.5cm (1in) chunks

3 tablespoons olive oil

1 red pepper, cored, deseeded and cut into 2cm (¾in) chunks

1 small courgette, cut into 2cm (¾in) chunks

1 red onion, thickly sliced

2 celery sticks, cut into 15mm (⅝in) pieces

2–3 garlic cloves, minced

100g (3½oz) cherry tomatoes, halved

2 tablespoons tomato purée

3 tablespoons red wine vinegar

1 tablespoon caster sugar

1 tablespoon capers, drained

2 tablespoons sultanas

6 green olives, pitted and roughly chopped

320g (11¼oz) farfalle

Salt and pepper

Handful of basil leaves, torn if large, to serve

Preheat the oven to 200°C (400°F), Gas Mark 6.

Toss the aubergine with 1 tablespoon of the oil and spread out evenly on a baking tray. Toss the red pepper and courgette together with 1 tablespoon of the oil and spread out on another baking tray. Roast for 25–30 minutes, turning halfway through to cook evenly.

When the vegetables have been roasting for 15 minutes, warm a large, deep frying pan and add the remaining oil. Cook the onion and celery for 10 minutes, then add the garlic and cook for a further 1 minute. Add the cherry tomatoes and cook for 5 minutes.

Add the roasted vegetables, then the tomato purée, vinegar, sugar, capers, sultanas and olives and cook for a further 2 minutes.

Meanwhile, bring a saucepan of water to the boil, add salt and cook the pasta for 9–10 minutes, or until al dente, then drain.

Toss the pasta with the sauce, adjust the seasoning to taste, divide between bowls and serve scattered with basil leaves.

vermicelli with cherry tomatoes, rocket and feta

This is a lovely dish that balances salty olives, tangy limes and creamy feta cheese. I love kaffir lime leaves; they really bring out the sunshine flavour of lime. Be sure to slice them super thin, then chop so they resemble zest. In a pinch, you can substitute lime zest, but I find it a little bitter. Vermicelli varies depending on country and brand – in Italy it is often slightly thicker than spaghetti, but in other countries it can be slightly thinner, more like angel hair. If you can't find vermicelli, then simply use spaghetti or any other long, thin pasta variety.

Serves 4

Carbs 61g   Sugar 4g   Protein 14g   Fibre 6g   Fat 16g   Sat Fat 4g   Salt 1.2g

300g (11¼oz) vermicelli
1 tablespoon olive oil
2 garlic cloves, sliced
2 tablespoons smoked rapeseed oil (or olive oil)
3 tablespoons lime juice
200g (7oz) Oven-dried Tomatoes (see page 29)
30g (1oz) pickled jalapeño peppers, roughly chopped
70g (2½oz) Nocellara olives, pitted and roughly chopped
Salt and pepper

To serve
70g (2½oz) feta, crumbled
2 kaffir lime leaves, very thinly shredded then chopped
60g (2¼oz) rocket, shredded

Bring a saucepan of water to the boil, add salt and cook the pasta for 9–10 minutes, or until al dente.

Meanwhile, warm a large, deep frying pan over a medium heat and cook the olive oil and garlic together for 1 minute until golden. Remove from the heat. Whisk the smoked rapeseed oil, lime juice and some pepper into the oil and garlic.

Drain the pasta and add it to the pan, then add the oven-dried tomatoes, jalapeño peppers and olives and toss everything together.

Serve up in bowls with the feta, lime leaves and rocket scattered on top.

mafaldine with romanesco sauce and lemon

Traditionally, this is made with romanesco, a brassica found in Italy, but you could use regular broccoli if you prefer the texture, although it is less creamy. Romanesco tastes like a cross between cauliflower and broccoli. I love it. It breaks down and forms a lovely low-calorie but rich-tasting sauce.

Serves 4 calories 444

Carbs 62g   Sugar 4.5g   Protein 20g   Fibre 10g   Fat 11g   Sat Fat 3g   Salt 0.2g

600g (1lb 5oz) romanesco, broken into florets
2 tablespoons olive oil
2–3 garlic cloves, chopped
½ teaspoon dried chilli flakes
320g (11¼oz) mafaldine or other long-cut pasta
40g (1½oz) Parmesan, grated
Salt and pepper
1 lemon, cut into wedges, to serve

Bring a medium saucepan of water to the boil and cook the romanesco for 5–6 minutes until tender. Drain.

Bring a separate large saucepan of water to the boil, add salt and cook the pasta for 6–7 minutes, or until al dente. Drain, reserving some of the cooking water.

Warm the oil in a large, deep frying pan over a medium heat and cook the garlic for 1–2 minutes. Add the chilli flakes and romanesco and cook for 4 minutes, smashing up a few florets for texture.

Add the warm cooked pasta and three-quarters of the grated Parmesan to the frying pan with a little of the pasta water and stir.

Serve with the remaining Parmesan, a grinding of pepper and the lemon wedges.

spelt penne alla norma

This is another classic Sicilian pasta dish. You can make it with Pecorino Romano or Parmesan, but the classic version uses ricotta salata — one of my favourites. Do try and find it if you can as the flavour is quite different. You can find it at most Italian delis or supermarkets.

Serves 4 calories 451

Carbs 68g   Sugar 11g   Protein 14.5g   Fibre 9g   Fat 12g   Sat Fat 2g   Salt 0.2g

2 firm medium aubergines (about 700g/1lb 9oz), cut into large chunks
3 tablespoons olive oil
3 garlic cloves, minced
1 teaspoon oregano
¼ teaspoon dried chilli flakes
2 teaspoons red wine vinegar
500g (1lb 2oz) passata
300g (11¼oz) spelt penne or other short-cut pasta
Salt and pepper

To serve
2 sprigs of basil, leaves shredded
40g (1½oz) ricotta salata, shaved

Preheat the oven to 200°C (400°F), Gas Mark 6.

Toss the aubergine and 2 tablespoons of the oil together, spread out on baking trays and roast for 20 minutes, until soft and golden. When cooked, set aside.

Add the remaining 1 tablespoon of oil to a large, deep frying pan and cook the garlic for 1 minute. Stir in the roasted aubergine, oregano, chilli flakes and vinegar and cook for 1 minute. Add the passata and simmer for 15 minutes.

Meanwhile, bring a large saucepan of water to the boil, add salt and cook the pasta for 9 minutes, or until al dente.

Drain the pasta, reserving some of the cooking water. Add the pasta to the sauce and toss to coat, adding a little pasta water to the sauce if it is too thick.

Serve in bowls, sprinkled with the shredded basil, shaved ricotta salata and some pepper.

lasagne with beluga lentil sauce

I absolutely adore beluga lentils. Add them to a marinara sauce and you've got a wonderful vegetarian Bolognese. I promise you won't miss the meat in this lasagna. You could also make it with mushrooms instead of lentils; just substitute 300g (10½oz) sautéed mushrooms and add a dash of Worcestershire sauce.

Serves 6 calories 423

Carbs 41g   Sugar 8g   Protein 24g   Fibre 7.5g   Fat 15g   Sat Fat 8g   Salt 0.7g

6 lasagna sheets
250g (9oz) ricotta
1 egg, beaten
30g (1oz) Pecorino Romano, grated
1 quantity Lean Bolognese Sauce using the lentils (see page 27)
125g (4½oz) mozzarella, shredded, 50g (1¾oz) split for the layers and 25g (1oz) for the topping
Black pepper

Preheat the oven to 220°C (425°F), Gas Mark 7.

Meanwhile, soak the lasagna sheets in warm water for 15 minutes.

Mix the ricotta and egg together with 20g (¾oz) of the Pecorino Romano.

Ladle some of the tomato and lentil sauce into the base of a 20cm (8in) square baking dish. Place 2 sheets of lasagna on top then half the ricotta filling, a few ladles of sauce and 50g (1¾oz) of mozzarella. Repeat these layers, then top with the remaining 2 lasagna sheets, the remainder of the sauce and both cheeses.

Cover with foil and bake for 40 minutes, then remove the foil and bake for a further 10–20 minutes, until the lasagna is tender and golden. Season with black pepper and serve.

Linguine lunghi with herbs, green olives and lemon

This dish is loaded with an assortment of fresh herbs and the combination of fruity olive oil and creamy butter, and then finished with some pickled jalapeño peppers. I know it sounds a bit unconventional, but the added heat of the jalapeño and the acidity of the vinegar help to round out the dish while the saltiness of the cheese completes it.

Serves 4 calories 488

Carbs 58g   Sugar 2.5g   Protein 15g   Fibre 5g   Fat 21g   Sat Fat 7g   Salt 1g

320g (11¼oz) linguine
2 tablespoons olive oil
2 tablespoons butter
3 anchovies, tinned in oil
2 garlic cloves, sliced
60g (2¼oz) Nocellara olives,
   pitted and roughly chopped
30g (1oz) pickled jalapeño
   pepper, chopped
1 tablespoon lemon zest
1–2 tablespoons lemon juice
5 sprigs of dill, roughly
   chopped
20g (¾oz) parsley, stems
   removed, leaves chopped
10g (¼oz) sprigs of tarragon,
   leaves roughly chopped
20g (¾oz) coriander, roughly
   chopped
Salt and pepper

To serve
15g (½oz) smoked almonds,
   roughly chopped
40g (1½oz) Pecorino Romano,
   grated

Bring a saucepan of water to the boil, add salt and cook the pasta for 9–10 minutes, or until al dente.

Meanwhile, heat a large, deep frying pan over a medium heat and add the oil and butter. Add the anchovies, mashing them so they break down, and the garlic and cook for a further 1 minute. Turn off the heat.

Drain the pasta, reserving some of the cooking water. Add the pasta to the frying pan with the olives, jalapeño pepper and lemon zest and juice. Add the herbs and some pepper and toss through.

Divide among 4 bowls and top with the smoked almonds and grated cheese, to serve.

gluten-free gnocchi with roasted butternut squash, brown butter and sage

The addition here of pomegranate seeds rounds off the sweetness of the squash and nuttiness of the butter with just the right amount of acid and tang. Plus, it is a lovely colourful garnish to lift the dish.

Serves 4

Carbs 55g   Sugar 6g   Protein 10.5g   Fibre 5g   Fat 16.5g   Sat Fat 7g   Salt 0.6g

300g (10½oz) butternut squash flesh, cut into small chunks
2 tablespoons olive oil
1 quantity Gluten-free Gnocchi (see page 23)
2 tablespoons butter
5 sage leaves, chopped
40g (1½oz) Parmesan, grated
40g (1½oz) pomegranate seeds, to garnish

Preheat the oven to 200°C (400°F), Gas Mark 6.

Toss the squash with half of the olive oil and spread out evenly on a baking tray. Roast for 30–35 minutes.

Meanwhile, make and cook the gnocchi. Drain, reserving some of the cooking water, and set aside.

Put the remaining oil and the butter in a deep frying pan and cook for 1–2 minutes until browned and it smells nutty. Add the gnocchi and sauté for 2 minutes, then add the roasted squash, sage and a splash of pasta cooking water and toss together.

Serve on plates topped with grated Parmesan and pomegranate seeds.

cacio y pepe

Once you master this simple cheese and pepper sauce dish, you will want to make it over and over again. The key is to work quickly, stirring the cheese and pasta water through the pasta so it doesn't get clumpy. It is classically made with Pecorino Romano cheese, but you could use Parmesan at a pinch. This can easily be made vegan by substituting vegan butter and Parmesan.

Serves 4 calories 466

· ·

Carbs 58g   Sugar 2g   Protein 21g   Fibre 4g   Fat 15g   Sat Fat 8g   Salt 0.6g

· ·

320g (11¼oz) spaghetti
1 tablespoon olive oil
1 tablespoon butter
2–3 teaspoons cracked black
    pepper
120g (4¼oz) Pecorino
    Romano, finely grated and
    kept at room temperature, as
    it blends into the sauce better
Salt

Bring a large saucepan of water to the boil, add salt and cook the pasta for 8 minutes, or until al dente. Halfway through cooking, scoop out 200ml (7fl oz) of the pasta water and set aside.

Place a large, deep frying pan over a medium heat and add the oil and butter. When the butter has melted, add the pepper and turn down the heat to low. Pour in about half of the reserved pasta water, then turn off the heat.

Add the drained pasta and keep stirring, gradually adding 100g (3½oz) of the grated cheese, until the sauce is creamy and the pasta is thoroughly coated. Add more pasta water as necessary; it should be creamy but not swimming in sauce.

Divide among 4 bowls and serve immediately, sprinkled with the remaining 20g (¾oz) of grated cheese.

pasta arrabbiata

This simple recipe can be thrown together in minutes and is perfect for
a weeknight meal. All you have to do is chop some chillies and garlic and
open a couple of cans of tomatoes — it's that easy! The tubular shape
of the ziti holds the sauce really well.

Serves 4 calories 436

Carbs 65g   Sugar 9.5g   Protein 17g   Fibre 6g   Fat 11g   Sat Fat 3.5g   Salt 0.3g

2 tablespoons olive oil
2 garlic cloves, chopped
2 red chillies, deseeded and
   finely chopped
1 tablespoon tomato purée
2 x 400g (14oz) cans good-
   quality plum tomatoes
320g (11¼oz) ziti
Salt and pepper

To serve
50g (1¾oz) Parmesan, grated
Handful of basil leaves, torn
   if large

Heat 1 tablespoon of the oil in a large, deep frying pan,
add the garlic and chillies and cook for 1–2 minutes.
Stir in the tomato purée and add the plum tomatoes
too, squishing them in your hand to break them down.
Adjust the seasoning and simmer for 20 minutes.

Meanwhile, bring a saucepan of water to the boil, add
salt and cook the pasta for 9–10 minutes, or until al
dente. Drain.

Toss the pasta in the tomato sauce then divide among 4
serving dishes, drizzle with the remaining 1 tablespoon
of olive oil and scatter over the Parmesan and basil
leaves, to serve.

orecchiette with cime di rapa and chilli

Cime di rapa, turnips greens, broccoli rabe or rapini — whatever you call it, it is delicious. This bitter green vegetable is a member of the turnip family and is a match made in heaven when combined with pasta, garlic, grassy olive oil and a touch of heat from chilli.

Serves 4 calories 453

Carbs 61g   Sugar 4g   Protein 18g   Fibre 8.5g   Fat 13g   Sat Fat 3.5g   Salt 0.2g

450–500g (1lb–1lb 2oz) cime di rapa
320g (11¼oz) orecchiette
3 tablespoons olive oil
3–4 garlic cloves, minced
½ teaspoon dried chilli flakes
Salt and pepper
40g (1½oz) Pecorino Romano, grated, to serve

Discard the tough, thicker stalks of the cime di rapa and cut the remainder into 2cm (¾in) pieces. Separate the florets and cut them in half if large.

Bring a large saucepan of water to the boil, add salt and cook the pasta for 6–8 minutes, and 2 minutes before the pasta is ready, add the cime de rapa. Drain, reserving some of the pasta water.

Put the oil into a large, deep frying pan and cook the garlic for 1 minute. Add the chilli flakes, pasta and cime di rapa. Stir through and add a little pasta water if needed. Adjust the seasoning to taste.

Serve in bowls, topped with the grated cheese.

calamarata pasta with roasted red onion and radicchio

Roasting the onions and grapes brings out all the sweetness locked inside, which is yin to the yang of the bitterness of the radicchio and saltiness of the cheese.

Serves 4

Carbs 72g   Sugar 14g   Protein 15g   Fibre 7g   Fat 12g   Sat Fat 4g   Salt 0.3g

4 small red onions (about 400g/14oz), quartered, but unpeeled
1 tablespoon + 2 teaspoons olive oil
125g (4½oz) red grapes
320g (11¼oz) calamarata pasta (thick ringed)
60g (2¼oz) soft goats' cheese
½ small head of radicchio, leaves shredded
Salt and pepper

To serve
2 tablespoons aged balsamic vinegar of Modena
15g (½oz) walnuts, toasted
1 sprig of rosemary leaves, chopped

Preheat the oven to 200°C (400°F), Gas Mark 6.

Toss the onions with the 2 teaspoons of olive oil, place on a baking tray and roast for 25–30 minutes until golden. Spread the grapes out on another tray and place in the oven 10 minutes before the onions are cooked.

Remove the onions and grapes from the oven, drain and reserve the juice released by the grapes. Leave the onions to cool slightly, then then cut off the root ends and remove the skins.

Bring a saucepan of water to the boil, add salt and cook the pasta for 12–14 minutes, or until al dente. Drain, reserving some of the pasta water.

Add the remaining 1 tablespoon of oil to a large, deep frying pan and toss the onions into the pan, stirring for a few minutes. Add the pasta, goats' cheese, reserved grape juices and some pasta water and stir until creamy. Season and stir through the radicchio and grapes.

Serve in bowls, topped with a drizzle of balsamic vinegar, the walnuts and rosemary.

wheat tagliatelle with mushroom and kalettes

Mushrooms are a wonderful alternative to meat if you are vegetarian. Their earthy flavour and fleshy texture are enough for me to pass on meat — especially when they are sautéed in good olive oil and a touch of butter. Kalettes are a cross between kale and Brussels sprouts and make a wonderful addition to this earthy dish. If you can't find them, regular kale will do.

Serves 4 calories 497

Carbs 58g Sugar 4.5g Protein 19g Fibre 13g Fat 18g Sat Fat 7g Salt 0.4g

15g (½oz) dried porcini mushrooms
2 tablespoons olive oil
1 small shallot, finely diced
3 garlic cloves, minced
2 tablespoons butter
300g (10½oz) mixed fresh wild mushrooms, cut into bite-sized pieces
150g (5½oz) kalettes, hard base removed, leaves shredded, or kale, shredded if you can't find kalettes
350g (12½oz) fresh wholemeal tagliatelle
Salt and pepper

To serve
2 sprigs of thyme, leaves picked
40g (1½oz) Parmesan, grated
1 lemon, cut into wedges

Soak the dried porcini mushrooms in 200ml (7fl oz) hot water for 15 minutes. Drain, reserving the liquid. Remove any grit from the mushrooms, then chop.

Warm 1 tablespoon of the oil in a large, deep frying pan and cook the shallot for 2–3 minutes. Add the garlic and cook for 1 minute more, then remove from the pan and set aside. Add 1 tablespoon of the butter and the remaining 1 tablespoon of oil to the pan and, when the butter has melted, add the mixed wild mushrooms and cook, stirring, for 5 minutes. Add the porcini and half of the reserved soaking liquid and reduce until slightly thick. Add the kalettes or kale and cook for 2–3 minutes.

Meanwhile, bring a saucepan of salted water to the boil and cook the pasta for 2–3 minutes, or until al dente.

Add the pasta to the frying pan and mix. Finish by stirring through the remaining butter, the remaining porcini soaking liquid and the shallot and garlic mixture. Stir well, and season with salt and pepper.

Serve in bowls, scattered with thyme leaves and grated Parmesan, with lemon wedges alongside.

strozzapreti with artichoke hearts, broad beans and peas

Artichokes are my favourite vegetable; they just shout spring is here.
They can be a lot of work to clean and cook, but it's worth it for the
delicious results. Here, however, all the hard work has been
done for you with pre-charred artichokes. You can find them
in most supermarkets now, they are divine on a pizza as well
as luscious in this pasta dish.

Serves 4 calories 498

Carbs 55g Sugar 4g Protein 19g Fibre 9g Fat 20g Sat Fat 8g Salt 1.3g

1 tablespoon olive oil
2 tablespoons butter
4 spring onions, thinly sliced,
   whites and greens separated
3 garlic cloves, sliced
350g (12½oz) fresh
   strozzapreti
175g (6oz) charred artichokes,
   sliced
100g (5½oz) broad beans,
   shelled and peeled weight
100g (3½oz) peas
Salt and pepper

To garnish and serve
1 lemon, cut into wedges
40g (1½oz) Parmesan, grated
Handful of basil leaves, torn

Warm a large, deep frying pan over a medium heat
and add the oil and 1 tablespoon of the butter. When
the butter has melted, add the spring onion whites and
cook for 3 minutes, then add the garlic and cook for
1–2 minutes.

Meanwhile, bring a saucepan of water to the boil.
Add salt and cook the pasta for 2 minutes, then add the
broad beans and peas and cook for a further 2 minutes,
or until the pasta al dente. Drain, reserving some of
the cooking water.

Add the pasta, broad beans and peas to the onion
and garlic along with the artichokes, then stir in the
remaining butter and the reserved cooking water
if necessary. Adjust the seasoning to taste.

Serve, garnished with lemon wedges, and topped with
grated Parmesan, basil and spring onion greens.

pointed spring cabbage with noodles, toasted butter and micro sorrel

The first time I had pointed cabbage with butter and almonds was
on a shoot. I have always loved butter and cabbage, but add the almonds
and it was so delicious I couldn't stop eating it. I thought,
I'm going to make this again with pasta! So I slimmed it down and added
sorrel and lemon to bite through the fat of the butter. Smoked almonds add
a lovely flavour element, but you could also use plain roasted nuts. Cooking
the butter until it gets brown brings out a real nutty flavour.
The French call it *beurre noisette* or brown butter.

Serves 4

Carbs 60g   Sugar 7.5g   Protein 16g   Fibre 8g   Fat 19g   Sat Fat 7g   Salt 0.5g

400g (14oz) fresh pappardelle
1 tablespoon olive oil
3 tablespoons butter
1 small head of pointed
   cabbage, quartered
   and sliced
Salt and pepper

To serve and garnish
30g (1oz) toasted smoked
   almonds, chopped
Micro sorrel, if available,
   to garnish, or regular
   sorrel, shredded
1 lemon, cut into wedges

Bring a large saucepan of water to the boil, add salt and
cook the noodles for 3–4 minutes, or until al dente,
then drain.

Warm a large, deep frying pan, add the oil and butter
and cook, stirring, until it goes slightly brown and
toasted. Add the cabbage and sauté until wilted,
caramelized and soft but still with a bit of crunch.
You may need to do this in a few batches.

Toss the pasta with the cabbage, adjust the seasoning
to taste, and serve in bowls, topped with the almonds
and sorrel and with lemon wedges alongside.

mafaldine pasta prima vera

This dish is delicious in the spring when asparagus and broad beans come into season. It is vibrant and green — just like the grass after an April shower in your garden, when flowers are blooming and hopes of summer days are not too far away.

Serves 4   calories 498

Carbs 61g   Sugar 5g   Protein 18g   Fibre 9g   Fat 18g   Sat Fat 8g   Salt 0.3g

300g (10½oz) long pasta of your choice, such as mafaldine
2 tablespoons olive oil
2 spring onions, sliced
1 carrot, peeled and diced
2 garlic cloves, minced
100g (3½oz) tenderstem broccoli, cut into bite-sized pieces
100g (3½oz) asparagus tips, sliced
1 tablespoon butter
100g (3½oz) broad beans, shelled weight
50g (1 ¾oz) shelled fresh peas (frozen are fine too)
100ml (3½fl oz) single cream
Salt and pepper

To serve
1 tablespoon each chopped oregano, basil and parsley
40g (1½oz) Pecorino Romano, grated or shaved
Few edible flowers

Bring a saucepan of water to the boil, add salt and cook the pasta for 5–7 minutes, or until al dente. Drain, reserving some of the cooking water.

Warm a large, deep frying pan, add 1 tablespoon of the oil, the spring onions and carrot and sauté for 2–3 minutes. Add the garlic and cook for 1 minute. Add the broccoli and asparagus and cook for 2 minutes. Add the butter and the remaining 1 tablespoon of oil, along with the pasta, peas, broad beans and cream. Loosen with a little of the pasta water if needed and cook for 2 minutes, then season to taste.

Serve in bowls, sprinkled with the herbs, grated or shaved cheese and the edible flowers.

spaghetti with oil, garlic and chilli

This is quick and easy to throw together and is also super healthy: delicious fruity olive oil is good for your heart and skin, garlic is known for its antibacterial properties, and chillies are full of vitamins and antioxidants. Since chillies vary in heat, be sure to taste them before using.

Serves 4 calories 430

Carbs 58g   Sugar 2g   Protein 13.5g   Fibre 4g   Fat 15g   Sat Fat 4g   Salt 0.2g

320g (11¼oz) long pasta
4 tablespoons olive oil
4–5 garlic cloves, finely
   chopped
½ teaspoon dried chilli flakes,
   or 1–2 fresh red chillies,
   deseeded and sliced
40g (1½oz) Parmesan or
   Pecorino Romano, grated
3 tablespoons chopped parsley
A drizzle of aged balsamic
   vinegar of Modena (optional)

Bring a saucepan of water to the boil, add salt and cook the pasta until al dente. Drain, reserving at least 100ml (3½fl oz) of the cooking water.

Heat a large, deep frying pan over a medium heat and warm the oil for 1 minute. Turn off the heat and add the garlic and chilli flakes or chillies. Stir, then leave to sit for 2 minutes.

Add the pasta to the pan and stir to coat. Add a little of the reserved pasta water if needed.

Serve in bowls, sprinkled with the grated Parmesan or Pecorino Romano cheese and chopped parsley. Although it's not traditional, drizzle over some aged balsamic vinegar to round out the flavour.

fish and meat mains

If you go to an Italian restaurant you are likely to find most of these dishes on the menu, but I've lost count of the times I've been out with a friend and heard them say, "Oh, geez, I'd love to have the carbonara, but the calories will kill me!" By slimming the recipes down through clever swaps, portion control and using fresh, quality ingredients, you can have your favourite pasta main course with your favourite sauce as I've done the hard bit for you.

Cured meats are so packed with flavour that only a small portion is necessary to bring out their essence. They are used here more like a condiment, intended to accentuate and complement — pancetta in Bucatini al'Amatriciana (see page 149) creates a smoky backdrop to the sweet tomatoes, while thinly sliced ham, baked until crisp and crumbly, are an easy way to flavour an entire dish with just a sprinkling.

Fresh seafood also has a wonderful richness when paired with pasta. Clams are ideal for a weeknight dinner — they bring the taste of the ocean and require very little seasoning. Anchovies are fantastic for imparting smoky and salty undertones too, and it only requires a few to be mashed up and cooked in olive oil to season a dish, such as in Puttanesca (see page 131). Paired with tomatoes, capers and olives, it makes a sauce bursting with aroma.

So put your apron on, pour yourself a glass of wine, turn on some tunes and have fun cooking.

maltagliati with smoked salmon, crème fraiche and dill

Maltagliati — "poorly cut" in Italian — is made by cutting fresh pasta dough into irregular shapes. It can also be made by breaking up pieces of lasagna. I always find I have leftover broken sheets of lasagna that just sit in the box — now they have a purpose.

Serves 4 calories 491

Carbs 46g   Sugar 3g   Protein 24.5g   Fibre 3g   Fat 23g   Sat Fat 10g   Salt 1.6g

325g (11½oz) fresh maltagliati
   (or 260g/9oz dried)
125g (5½oz) crème fraîche
200g (7oz) smoked salmon,
   roughly chopped
2 tablespoons each chopped
   dill and chives
Salt and pepper

To serve
50g (1¾oz) salmon roe
2 lemons, 1 zested, 1 cut
   into wedges

Bring a saucepan of water to the boil, add salt and cook the pasta for 2–3 minutes (allow 8–9 minutes if you're using dried pasta), or until al dente.

Drain the pasta, then stir and warm through the crème fraîche, smoked salmon and herbs. Season with salt and pepper.

Divide among 4 bowls, top with the salmon roe and lemon zest and serve with lemon wedges.

pasta with tuna, capers and black olives

This is definitely a pantry pasta dish. If I've been working all day and don't feel like dragging myself to the shops, I can whip this up from what is in my cupboard. The olives could be green and you can replace the parsley with basil if you prefer.

Serves 4

Carbs 59g   Sugar 2.5g   Protein 21g   Fibre 4.5g   Fat 14g   Sat Fat 2g   Salt 0.6vg

320g (11¼oz) long pasta, such as spaghetti or vermicelli
3 tablespoons olive oil
2 anchovies, tinned in oil and drained, roughly chopped
3 garlic cloves, minced
½ teaspoon chilli flakes
160g (5¾oz) can Italian albacore tuna, drained and flaked
100g (3 ½oz) oven-dried tomatoes, chopped (see page 29)
2 tablespoons small capers, drained
50g (1¾oz) black olives, pitted and chopped
10g (¼oz) parsley leaves
Salt and pepper
1 lemon, cut into wedges, to serve

Bring a saucepan of water to the boil, add salt and cook the pasta for 9–10 minutes, or until al dente. Drain, reserving some of the cooking water.

Warm a large, deep frying pan, add 2 tablespoons of the oil and cook the anchovies for 1 minute, breaking them up. Add the garlic and cook for 1 minute, then add the chilli flakes and pasta and stir to combine, adding a little of the pasta water if needed. Stir in the tuna, tomatoes, capers, olives and parsley and cook for 2 minutes. Season with pepper.

Serve in bowls or plates with lemon wedges.

spaghetti puttanesca

This dish has lots of colourful tales behind it, but it's basically a quick pasta dish that can be thrown together for dinner without too much fuss. It calls for black olives. When I say black, I don't mean the ready-pitted kind you put on your fingers as a kid, though they have their place. I mean lovely meaty black olives, almost purple in colour, like Gaeta, Leccino or Ligurian. You could also use Kalamata at a pinch.

Serves 4

Carbs 64g　Sugar 8g　Protein 13g　Fibre 5g　Fat 10g　Sat Fat 1.5g　Salt 0.6g

320g (11¼oz) spaghetti
2 tablespoons olive oil
2 garlic cloves, chopped
4–5 anchovies, tinned in oil
　and drained
½ teaspoon dried chilli flakes,
　more if you like it really spicy
2 tablespoons tomato purée
500g (1lb 2oz) passata
200g (7oz) chopped tomatoes
75g (2¾oz) black olives, pitted
　and roughly chopped
1½ tablespoons salted capers,
　rinsed and chopped
Salt and pepper
2 tablespoons chopped parsley,
　to serve

Bring a saucepan of water to the boil, add salt and cook the spaghetti for 9–11 minutes, or until al dente, then drain.

Warm a large, deep frying pan over a very low heat and add the oil. Sauté the garlic and anchovies together, breaking up the anchovies; as they cook, they will dissolve and flavour the oil. Add the chilli flakes and tomato purée and cook for 1–2 minutes before adding the passata and chopped tomatoes. Simmer for 5 minutes. Add the olives and capers and cook for an additional 1–2 minutes.

Add the pasta to the sauce and toss. Serve in bowls with the chopped parsley and some freshly ground black pepper.

linguine con le vongole

This recipe is full of the ocean's briny goodness. I like to add a touch of butter at the end to round out the brine, and plenty of lemon to squeeze over and finish. A local fishmonger or supermarket fish counter should have clams that have already been purged of sand; if not, soak them in cold salted water for about 20 minutes and give them a scrub before using.

Serves 4 calories 464

Carbs 61g   Sugar 2g   Protein 24g   Fibre 4g   Fat 11g   Sat Fat 5g   Salt 2.9g

320g (11¼oz) linguine
1 tablespoon olive oil
7 garlic cloves, thinly sliced
½ teaspoon chilli flakes, plus
 extra for serving (optional)
1kg (2lb 4oz) clams, cleaned
100ml (3½fl oz) dry white wine
2 tablespoons cold butter

To serve
4 tablespoons chopped parsley
1 lemon, cut into wedges

Bring a saucepan of water to the boil and cook the pasta for 9–10 minutes, or until al dente. There is no need to add salt to the water as the clams will already be very salty. Drain, reserving about 100ml (3½fl oz) of the pasta water.

Pour the oil into a large, deep frying pan and sauté the garlic over a low heat for 2 minutes. Add the chilli flakes, clams and wine, cover and cook for 5 minutes or so, until all the clams are opened. Remove the clams using a slotted spoon and discard any that did not open. Set aside and cover.

Whisk the butter into the clam liquor and simmer for 3 minutes. Add the linguine to the pan with the reserved pasta water and cook for 2 minutes. Add the clams back to the pan and toss.

Divide among 4 pasta bowls, sprinkle with the parsley and extra chilli flakes, if using, and serve with the lemon wedges.

spaghetti with cornish crab, lemon, chilli and coriander

I use a mix of dark and white Cornish crab meat in this dish because I like how the dark meat is almost like cream in texture and tends to have a deeper flavour. It forms a lovely sauce with the wine and olive oil.

Serves 4

Carbs 59g   Sugar 3g   Protein 23g   Fibre 4.5g   Fat 14g   Sat Fat 2g   Salt 0.6g

320g (11¼oz) spaghetti
4 tablespoons olive oil
2 garlic cloves, minced
½ teaspoon chilli flakes, or
　1 red chilli, finely chopped,
　plus more for garnish if you
　like it spicy
150g (5½oz) cherry tomatoes
100ml (3½fl oz) dry white wine
250g (9oz) Cornish crab meat
　(50g (1¾oz) brown and
　200g (7oz) white)
1 tablespoon capers, drained
　and roughly chopped
4 tablespoons chopped
　coriander
Salt and pepper
1 lemon, cut into wedges,
　to garnish

Bring a saucepan of water to the boil, add salt and cook the pasta for 9–10 minutes, or until al dente. Drain, reserving some of the cooking water.

Warm a large, deep frying pan over a medium heat, add 2 tablespoons of the oil and cook the garlic for 1 minute. Add the chilli and tomatoes and cook for 2 minutes.

Deglaze the pan with the wine and cook for 1–2 minutes. Stir in the crab meat, capers and pasta, adding a little pasta water if needed, and cook for 2 minutes. Stir in the coriander just before serving.

Serve in pasta bowls, drizzled with the remaining 2 tablespoons of olive oil, sprinkled with pepper and more chilli flakes, if you like, and garnished with lemon wedges.

chilli and garlic squid with squid ink pasta

The key to squid is not to overcook it. You can either cook it slowly for a long time over a low heat, or quickly in a hot pan. This dish is a quick one. I know some people find the black pasta a bit strange to the eye, but it is quite delicious to the taste buds.

Serves 4 calories 452 DF

Carbs 66g   Sugar 2g   Protein 21g   Fibre 4.5g   Fat 11g   Sat Fat 1.5g   Salt 0.3g

320g (11¼oz) squid ink pasta
3 tablespoons olive oil
3 garlic cloves, minced
3 tablespoons dried breadcrumbs
250g (9oz) baby squid, body cut into rings and tentacles intact, or 3 large tubes sliced into rings and tentacles intact
1 red chilli, deseeded and finely sliced, plus extra to garnish, (optional)
Salt and pepper
Handful of Greek basil leaves, to garnish
1 lemon, cut into wedges, to serve

Bring a saucepan of water to the boil, add salt and cook the pasta for 8–9 minutes, or until al dente. Drain, reserving some of the cooking water.

Add 1 tablespoon of the oil to a large, deep fring pan and cook the garlic and breadcrumbs for 1–2 minutes until golden. Remove and set aside.

Add the remaining oil to the hot pan and quickly stir-fry the squid for 2–3 minutes until golden. Remove the squid and set aside. Add half of the chilli and the pasta to the pan. Toss together, adding a little of the reserved pasta water if needed.

Serve in dishes, topped with the remaining chilli (if using), the basil and some cracked pepper, with lemon wedges alongside. Sprinkle with the garlic and breadcrumbs.

fiorelli with prawns, butter and tomatoes

I love the addition of butter to this sauce. It cuts through the tomato's tang and rounds it out nicely without adding too many calories. Since cheese is usually not the best marriage with seafood, the butter adds some depth.

Serves 4 calories 407

Carbs 61g   Sugar 5g   Protein 26g   Fibre 5g   Fat 14g   Sat Fat 6.5g   Salt 0.7g

1 tablespoon olive oil
3 garlic cloves, sliced
400g (14oz) can San Marzano
    plum tomatoes
320g (11¼oz) fiorelli
350g (12oz) raw tiger prawns,
    shelled
2–3 tablespoons butter
Salt and pepper
10g (¼oz) basil leaves,
    to garnish

Heat a large, deep frying pan over a medium heat, add the oil and garlic and cook for 1–2 minutes until golden. Break up the plum tomatoes with your hands and add to the garlic. Stir and simmer for 10 minutes, then season with salt and pepper.

Meanwhile, bring a saucepan of water to the boil, add salt and cook the pasta for 9–10 minutes, or until al dente. Drain, reserving some of the cooking water.

Add the prawns to the sauce and cook for 3 minutes, then toss in the pasta, adding a little of the pasta water to loosen if needed. Finish by stirring in the butter, coating every tube.

Serve in bowls, garnished with the basil.

Linguine with anchovies and lemon zest

As a child, I absolutely hated anchovies: to me they were what
"contaminated" pizza. My father, who loves anchovies, oil and garlic
on his pizza, would laugh at me as I made disgusted faces and picked them
off one by one. My palate has since graduated to a higher level and now
I really enjoy their smoky, salty goodness. You need only a few to enhance
a vinaigrette, pasta dish or pizza.

Serves 4 calories 424

Carbs 63g   Sugar 2g   Protein 12g   Fibre 4g   Fat 13g   Sat Fat 3g   Salt 0.3g

320g (11¼oz) linguine
2 tablespoons olive oil
1 tablespoon butter
4–5 anchovies, tinned in oil
   and drained
2 garlic cloves, minced
½ teaspoon chilli flakes
Salt and pepper

For the toasted breadcrumbs
1 tablespoon olive oil
30g (1oz) dried plain
   breadcrumbs
1 garlic clove, minced
1 tablespoon lemon zest

To serve
2 tablespoons chopped parsley
1 lemon, cut into wedges

Bring a saucepan of water to the boil, add salt and
cook the linguine for 9–10 minutes, or until al dente.
Drain, reserving some of the cooking water.

Meanwhile, make the toasted breadcrumbs. Heat the oil
in a large, deep frying pan, add the breadcrumbs and
sauté for a few minutes, then add the garlic and cook
for 1 minute more until golden. Remove from the pan,
stir in the lemon zest and set aside.

Wipe the pan clean, place back over a medium heat
and add the 2 tablespoons of oil with the butter and
anchovies. Cook for a few minutes, breaking up the
anchovies as they cook, then add the garlic and chilli
flakes and cook for a further minute.

Toss the cooked pasta into the anchovy mixture,
stirring in some of the reserved pasta water if needed.

Serve in pasta bowls, topped with the toasted
breadcrumbs and chopped parsley and with lemon
wedges alongside.

chicken paprikash
with fresh tagliatelle

Traditionally, this dish of Hungary is made with sweet paprika.
I've used half sweet paprika and half smoked paprika to wake
it up and add a bit of depth. It is perfect on a crisp winter's
night when you come in from the cold.

Serves 4 calories 484

Carbs 54g   Sugar 7g   Protein 44g   Fibre 4g   Fat 10g   Sat Fat 4g   Salt 1.2g

2 teaspoons grapeseed oil
1 sweet onion, thinly sliced
500g (1lb 2oz) chicken
   breasts
2 tablespoons tomato purée
1 tablespoon sweet paprika
1 tablespoon smoked paprika
1 chicken stock cube dissolved
   in 250ml (9fl oz) boiling
   water
1 red pepper, roasted (see page
   29, or from a jar) cut into
   thin strips
150g (5½oz) full-fat Greek
   yogurt
350g (12½oz) fresh tagliatelle
Salt and pepper
2 tablespoons chopped parsley,
   to serve

Add 1 teaspoon of the oil to a frying pan and cook the
onion for 5 minutes until golden and soft. Remove the
onion from the pan and set aside. Clean the pan.

Season the chicken breasts with salt and pepper and
add the remaining 1 teaspoon of oil to the pan. Sauté
the chicken for 3–4 minutes on each side. Remove the
chicken and place on a plate.

Add the tomato purée to the pan and cook for 1
minute, stirring, then add both paprikas and the stock
and stir. Return the chicken and onion to the pan, add
the red pepper and simmer for 5–7 minutes. Remove
the pan from the heat before slowly stirring in the
yogurt to prevent it from curdling.

Meanwhile, bring a large saucepan of water to the boil,
add salt and cook the tagliatelle for 3 minutes, or until
al dente, then drain.

Slice the chicken thinly and serve with the sauce over
the noodles, scattered with the chopped parsley.

orecchiette with broccoli, chicken sausage and harissa paste

This dish is a healthier version of your traditional sausage and broccoli because it is made with lean chicken. It still packs a lot of flavour into one meal especially with the zing of harissa and lemon.

Serves 4 calories 468

Carbs 61g   Sugar 3g   Protein 33g   Fibre 5g   Fat 9g   Sat Fat 3g   Salt 1.5g

250g (9oz) chicken sausages, removed from casings and cut into 2cm (¾in) chunks
320g (11¼oz) dried orecchiette or 400g (14oz) fresh
125g (4½oz) tenderstem broccoli, cut into bite-sized pieces
1 tablespoon olive oil
2–3 garlic cloves, sliced
2-3 tablespoons harissa paste
Salt and pepper

To serve

2 tablespoons chopped parsley
1 lemon, cut into wedges
40g (1½oz) Parmesan, grated, to serve

Sauté the chicken sausage chunks in a nonstick pan until cooked through, about 3–4 minutes. Drain on kitchen paper and set aside until needed.

Bring a saucepan of water to the boil, add salt and cook the pasta for 1–2 minutes less than the packet states, or until just al dente.

Add the broccoli to the pasta for the last 2 minutes of its cooking time. Drain, reserving a little of the cooking water.

Meanwhile, heat a frying pan over a medium heat, add the oil and garlic and cook for 1 minute, then remove from the heat.

Add the pasta, broccoli and sausage chunks to the pan and toss with the harissa paste and a little of the reserved pasta water.

Serve in bowls with a squeeze of lemon and a sprinkle of grated Parmesan and pepper.

chicken ragù and casarecce

Ragù is similar to Bolognese only it is made with chunks of meat rather than of minced meat. I've added pancetta for a touch of smoky flavour, but you could leave it out if you prefer just chicken. This makes a wonderful Sunday dinner served with a simple salad and a glass of red wine, when you don't want to fuss. The sauce can be made ahead of time and reheated.

Serves 4

Carbs 66g   Sugar 9g   Protein 24g   Fibre 6.5g   Fat 8g   Sat Fat 2g   Salt 0.8g

50g (1¾oz) diced pancetta
1 onion, finely diced
1 celery stick, finely diced
1 carrot, peeled and finely
 diced
2 garlic cloves, chopped
200g (7oz) boneless, skinless
 chicken thighs
100ml (3½fl oz) dry,
 full-bodied red wine
1 tablespoon red wine vinegar
250ml (9fl oz) chicken stock
400g (14oz) can crushed
 tomatoes
320g (11¼oz) dried casarecce
Salt and pepper

Heat a Dutch oven or heavy-gauge saucepan over a medium heat, add the pancetta, onion, celery and carrot and cook for 5 minutes. Add the garlic and cook for a further 1 minute.

Meanwhile, season the chicken with salt and pepper and brown in a separate nonstick pan for 3 minutes per side.

Add the chicken to the cooked vegetables along with the wine, vinegar, stock and tomatoes and simmer for 15 minutes. Pull the chicken apart with 2 forks as it becomes tender.

Meanwhile, bring a saucepan of water to the boil, add salt and cook the pasta for 9–11 minutes, or until al dente, then drain.

Divide the pasta between 4 dishes and pour over the chicken ragù sauce.

pasta with spinach, smoked chicken and ricotta

Ricotta is such a rich and creamy-tasting cheese, yet offers a light texture in a sauce as opposed to traditional thick, heavy cheese sauces. For a vegetarian version, omit the chicken and add some sautéed smoked tofu or mushrooms.

Serves 4

calories 488

Carbs 56g   Sugar 3g   Protein 32g   Fibre 4g   Fat 14g   Sat Fat 6.5g   Salt 0.4g

400g (14oz) fresh tagliatelle (or 320g/11¼oz dried)
2 teaspoons olive oil
2–3 garlic cloves, minced
160g (5¾oz) smoked chicken, diced
150g (5½oz) baby spinach, shredded
250g (9oz) ricotta
Salt and pepper

To serve
20g (¾oz) Pecorino Romano or Parmesan cheese, grated
Zest of 1 lemon
Few basil leaves (Greek basil if available)

Bring a saucepan of water to the boil, add salt and cook the fresh pasta for 3 minutes, or until al dente. If using dried pasta cook for 9–11 minutes. Drain, reserving some of the cooking water.

Pour the oil into a large, deep frying pan and cook the garlic for 1 minute. Add the chicken, spinach and 1 tablespoon of water and stir until the spinach has wilted, 1–2 minutes. Add the pasta and the ricotta along with a little of the pasta water and toss to coat all the pasta with the creamy cheese sauce. Season with pepper.

Serve with the grated cheese, lemon zest and basil.

spaghetti with carbonara and peas

The classic version of this dish contains guanciale or pancetta, eggs
and Parmesan or Pecorino Romano cheese. I've added peas for sweetness
and because that's how my little girl, Isla-Sophia, loves to eat it.
This is a carbonara that you could eat once a week and not feel guilty.

Serves 4
calories
493

Carbs 57g   Sugar 2g   Protein 26g   Fibre 5g   Fat 17g   Sat Fat 7g   Salt 1.2g

300g (10½oz) spaghetti
100g (3½oz) frozen peas
75g (2½oz) diced pancetta
3 large eggs
60g (2¼oz) Pecorino Romano
  cheese, grated
Salt and pepper
2 tablespoons roughly chopped
  parsley, to serve

Bring a saucepan of water to the boil, add salt and cook
the pasta for 9 minutes, or until al dente. Add the peas
2 minutes before the end of the cooking time. Drain,
reserving some of the pasta water.

Meanwhile, warm a large, deep frying pan over a
medium heat and cook the pancetta for 2–3 minutes.

Whisk the eggs and 60g (2¼oz) of the cheese together
with a pinch of salt and pepper. Set aside.

Add the pasta and peas to the pan of pancetta and give
it a good stir. Remove from the heat and slowly stir the
egg and cheese mixture into the pan using tongs or a
pasta fork, coating each strand, being careful not to
let it curdle. Add a little pasta water to thin it out and
make a shiny sauce.

Serve, sprinkled with the chopped parsley, remaining
cheese and a grinding of pepper.

bucatini al'amatriciana

The first time I tasted this dish was at a tiny restaurant in Little Italy
in Cleveland, Ohio. I absolutely loved it and have made it ever since.
I get so excited when a shop carries bucatini pasta. Traditionally, it is made
with guanciale, an Italian cured meat prepared with pork cheeks or jowl,
but this is quite fatty so I've substituted it with pancetta here. You can use
the rendered fat from the pancetta to cook the onion, so you don't
need to add oil.

Serves 4 calories 464

Carbs 66g   Sugar 10g   Protein 20g   Fibre 5g   Fat 11g   Sat Fat 4g   Salt 1g

320g (11¼oz) bucatini
75g (2¾oz) diced pancetta
1 small onion, diced
1–2 garlic cloves, chopped
½ teaspoon chilli flakes or
　1 small chilli, sliced, plus
　extra for serving (optional)
3 tablespoons tomato purée
100ml (3½fl oz) dry white wine
500g (1lb 2oz) passata or
　chopped tomatoes, blended
Salt and pepper
40g (1½oz) Pecorino Romano
　cheese, grated, to serve

Warm a large, deep frying pan, add the pancetta and
onion and cook for 5 minutes until brown. Add the
garlic and cook 1 minute. Add the chilli flakes and
tomato purée and cook for 1 minute, then pour in
the wine and cook for a further 1 minute. Tip in the
passata or tomatoes and simmer for 5 minutes.

Meanwhile, bring a saucepan of water to the boil,
add salt and cook the pasta for 6–8 minutes, or
until al dente.

Drain the pasta, reserving some of the cooking
water. Toss the pasta into the pan and cook for about
2 minutes, adding a little of the reserved pasta water
if needed to loosen.

Serve topped with grated Pecorino Romano cheese,
cracked pepper and more chilli flakes if you like
the heat.

warm antipasti pasta

Cooking the speck in this dish until it is crisp and crumbles is a great way to add a touch of smoky taste without too many calories. I've added a few typical antipasti ingredients to this simple pasta dish, so it's like eating your antipasti and pasta course all at the same time — a wonderful treat!

Serves 4 calories 500

Carbs 64g   Sugar 4g   Protein 19g   Fibre 6.5g   Fat 17.5g   Sat Fat 5g   Salt 2.5g

60g (2¼oz) Prosciutto di Speck
340g (12oz) mafalda corta, (short, wide, wavy ribbons), or farfalle
2 tablespoons olive oil
4 garlic cloves, sliced
½ teaspoon chilli flakes
Zest of 1 lemon and 2 tablespoons lemon juice
175g (6oz) charred artichoke hearts, drained and cut in half
200g (7oz) roasted peppers, jarred or homemade (see page 29)
6 Nocellara olives, pitted and chopped
Salt and pepper

To serve
40g (1½oz) rocket
25g (1oz) Parmesan, grated
Handful of basil leaves

Preheat the oven to 200°C (400°F), Gas Mark 6.

Put the speck on a nonstick mat and cook for 10–12 minutes, or until crispy. Remove and set aside. When cooled, crumble.

Bring a large saucepan of water to the boil, add salt and cook the pasta for 9–10 minutes, or until al dente. Drain, reserving some of the cooking water.

Place a large, deep frying pan over a medium-high heat and warm the oil. Add the garlic and chilli flakes and cook on low for 1–2 minutes. Add the pasta, lemon zest and juice, artichoke hearts, roasted peppers and olives and toss to mix, loosening with a little of the pasta water if needed.

Divide among 4 bowls and top with the rocket, crumbled speck, Parmesan, basil and a grinding of pepper, to serve.

meatballs with rigatoni and marinara sauce

Italians would never serve meatballs with spaghetti, despite the common misconception – spaghetti is simply too thin to mop up the rich sauce. A chunky pasta, such as rigatoni, is far more suitable. This was a Sunday staple in my Italian-American family; a saucepan of sauce would bubble away all day. This is a much lighter version of traditional egg heavy meatballs.

Serves 4 calories 500

Carbs 58g Sugar 9g Protein 30g Fibre 6.5g Fat 16g Sat Fat 5g Salt 0.4g

1 quantity of Marinara Sauce (see page 26), made with passata or crushed tomatoes
275g (9¾oz) rigatoni
A handful of basil leaves, torn, to garnish

For the meatballs
50g (1¾oz) low-fat sausagemeat
300g (11¼oz) organic minced beef, 12% fat
20g (¾oz) Pecorino Romano, grated, half reserved for serving
1 egg
½ teaspoon dried basil
½ teaspoon dried oregano
½ teaspoon dried parsley
Salt and pepper

Warm the marinara sauce in a pan.

Make the meatballs by mixing all the ingredients (less half the grated cheese) together in a bowl. Shape into 12 meatballs.

Place the meatballs into the sauce and cook over a medium-high heat for 15 minutes, stirring occasionally.

Meanwhile, bring a saucepan of water to the boil, add salt and cook the pasta for 9–12 minutes, or until al dente, then drain.

Divide the pasta among 4 bowls and top with the sauce and 3 meatballs per person.

Sprinkle with the cheese and the reserved basil and serve.

fusillone with sausage and tomato sauce

When I don't have time to go somewhere that stocks Italian sausage, or to my local Italian deli, I make this out of pork sausagemeat mixed with a combination of dried herbs. Sausagemeat contains a lot of calories, but there are healthier alternatives on the market, such as the British brand Heck.

Serves 4 calories 496

Carbs 63g   Sugar 9g   Protein 23g   Fibre 4.5g   Fat 16g   Sat Fat 6g   Salt 0.8g

¼ teaspoon each dried fennel seeds, oregano, basil, parsley, onion powder, garlic powder, paprika, salt and pepper

200g (7oz) low-fat sausagemeat (removed from casing if using sausages)

2 teaspoons olive oil

1 onion, diced

2 garlic cloves, minced

500g (1lb 2oz) passata

300g (10½oz) fusillone

Salt and pepper

To serve

3 tablespoons chopped parsley

40g (1½oz) Parmesan, grated

Chilli flakes

Toast all the herbs and seasonings in a small pan over a low heat then mix into the sausagemeat.

Brown the sausagemeat in a nonstick, deep frying pan, breaking it up with a wooden spoon. Drain off the fat and set the meat aside.

Add the oil to the pan with the onion and cook for 5 minutes, then add the garlic and passata, return the sausagemeat to the pan, season and simmer for 10 minutes.

Meanwhile, bring a saucepan of water to the boil, add salt and cook the pasta for 8–9 minutes, or until al dente. Drain, reserving some of the cooking water.

Add the pasta to the sauce and stir, adding a little of the pasta water if needed.

Serve in bowls sprinkled with parsley, gthe rated Parmesan and chilli.

index

resources

Most grocery stores will have many of the necessary ingredients used in this book, but for more specialised ingredients any local Italian deli is a good place to start. Online suppliers can also be a good option, with the added benefit of the ingredients being delivered straight to your door. Below are some suggestions.

Online suppliers

www.ocado.com

www.natoora.co.uk

www.italianfoodshop.co.uk

www.mattas.co.uk

www.valentinafinefoods.com

www.vallebona.co.uk

www.carluccios.com

www.gastronomica.co.uk

www.vinegarshed.com

www.eataly.com

www.wholefoodsmarket.com

Glossary for US

Aubergine – eggplant	Grill – broil/broiler
Beetroot – beet	Kitchen paper – paper towels
Borlotti beans – cranberry beans	Minced pork or lamb – ground pork or lamb
Broad bean – fava bean	Parchment paper – wax paper
Chicory – endive	Pea shoots – pea tendrils
Chilli flakes – red pepper flakes	Peppers – bell peppers
Coriander (fresh) – cilantro	Prawn – shrimp
Coriander (dried) – coriander	Pulses – legumes
Courgette – zucchini	Rocket – arugula
Frying pan – skillet	Spring onions – scallions

acknowledgements

So many people have poured their energy, time and passion into the creation of this book. Firstly, I'd like to thank my loving and ever-patient and supportive husband. He is always there pushing me to follow my dreams and never give up. Thanks to my adventurous, sweet little girl, Isla-Sophia who is my biggest cheerleader. I thank them both for being the best taste testers/guinea pigs for a good part of the year. Seems like every night I asked," Fancy pasta tonight?". Their honest feedback, backed up by sound advise and substitutions was most helpful. To my family for their constant love, support and encouragement to never settle and follow my dreams- thanks Mom and Dad, Brian, Jay, Jimmy, Annemarie, Jill and Sue and all my nieces-Hannah, Ellie, Sarah, Lucy and Lynne. To my great aunts on my dad's side of the family for passing down all your recipes and secrets to my mother, who cooks great Italian for an Irish woman. I can't forget my cousins, the Spiccia family for opening the delicious Italian Restaurant, Pizzazz, which played such a big part in so many family celebrations and influenced me to cook as a career.

To my wonderful friend, Teresa Mariano for being my sounding board, always.

Thanks to The Evans Family for being my guinea pigs all those nights and putting up with rounds of pasta courses. Michelle Heimburger for her creative and technical support as well.

To Judith Hannam for approaching me to write this book and guiding me through the process. Thanks to Angela Boggiano for encouraging me to go for it and live and breathe pasta for all those months.

To the lovely Hannah Coughlin for being on top of things and holding my hand throughout the entire process and being so patient — you are a star.

To Katie Giovanni who taught me all I know about food styling and whose constant love support and wisdom I'm grateful to have.

To Beatrice Ferrante for being my sounding board on all things culinary and Italian.

To Meghan Rogers for her wonderful advice and enthusiasm and passion for pasta.

To my wonderful testers Alice Ostan and Harriet Hudson, thanks for putting into words what I failed to convey at times and making sure the recipes translated from my mind to paper.

To my diligent assistant, Lola Milne for always being one step ahead of me and keeping me tidy, and always knowing where I put my tweezers. To Flossy McAsslan for her constant words of encouragement, perfect prepping and positive ray-of-sunshine attitude always. Harriet Hudson again, for your dedication, organizational skills and friendship over the years.

Thanks to Sophie Michell for all her enthusiasm and encouragement to write this book. Thanks to the always cheerful Tara O'Sullivan and the fabulous David Loftus for bringing me into the Kyle fold and working on Sophie's book which led me to my own.

Thanks to Anne McDowall for basically being a mind reader and turning some of my connect–the- dots thoughts into cohesive instructions. And Fiona Hunter for the expert nutritional analysis.

Tara Fisher for her fine tuned attention to details and stunning photography. And let's not forget, your wonderful sense of humour which made me laugh so many times. And Louise Leffler for her wonderful design that brought it all together.

Linda Berlin for her gorgeous propping from plates to wild flowers and styling. Her beautiful sense of style truly dressed up my recipes and made them shine.

To Jennifer Munro for all her care on the tech side of our shoots to making me coffee when I needed a jolt.

Kyle for starting Kyle Books, you are an amazing and inspirational woman.

To all the great chefs, stylist, writers and photographers out there whom have influenced me in subtle ways. I thank them.